CORPORATE LIFE IS HELL

HOW TO LIBERATE THE LEADER WITHIN YOU
AND BE HAPPY IN YOUR CAREER

MIKE CARACALAS

LIBERATED LEADERSHIP PRESS

ISBN: 978-1-7321673-1-5

Edited by Ameesha Green

Cover design by JD Smith Design

For my family

CONTENTS

INTRODUCTION

It's 8:00 on Monday morning and I'm about to walk into my boss's office. I didn't sleep at all last night and I can feel the anxiety rising in my gut. I have a feeling that this meeting isn't going to end well. The reason I couldn't sleep is that at 10:00 last night, yes—Sunday night, I received one of the worst emails I've ever gotten from a boss. Essentially, she let me know in no uncertain terms that she was unhappy with me. She also informed me that she had decided to move my team under one of my peers and take away virtually all of my responsibilities.

I've been around long enough to understand what this means. For more times than I care to remember, I've been on the other side, as the HR business partner to the executive who has decided to "manage out" their problem employee. As a matter of fact, I had personally witnessed the "managing out" of a few of my peers over the previous two years by this same boss.

As I lay awake all night thinking about this, stinging from the humiliation of her cowardly email, I felt absolutely horrible. This was not a position I ever imagined myself being in. Actually, let me correct that. I'm sure I did imagine it, at least in a general way, in the form of fearing something I wanted to avoid at all costs. Maybe it's more accurate to say I didn't *believe* it would ever happen to me. After all, I'd spent the past 20 years building a very successful corporate career. How could this be happening to me now?

Before I tell you what happens next, I want to tell you how I got here.

I never really knew what I wanted to be when I grew up. I went to college as an undeclared Freshman, which means I had no major. In school, I got lots of good advice, including the guidance not to worry about what kind of career I wanted, but rather to follow what interested me and then the career would follow. I was interested in everything in college, from Geology to Anthropology to Political Science, but the one major that finally grabbed me was Psychology. Since very early in my life, even back in elementary school, I was thinking about what was going on in my own head. Not only that, but I wondered a lot about what was going on in other people's heads, and whether it was anything like my own experience. I even remember thinking what it would be like if we could get inside each other's heads. Would it feel familiar? Or completely alien? Weird kid, huh? But I generally wanted to fit in and not be seen as weird, so I never voiced those ideas out loud. I guess I shouldn't have been surprised that following my interests resulted in a Bachelor's degree in Psychology.

Still, even when I graduated, I didn't know what I wanted to do, so I ended up in graduate school studying Organizational Psychology. The only logic behind this was that I figured it was the one field of Psychology where I might make the most money. I learned about Leadership, Change Management, Organization Design/Development, and Team Dynamics. Finally, I saw a career! I was going to *make Corporate America great!* And for the next 20 years, that's exactly what I did—or at least what I tried to do.

In the course of my career working inside Corporate America, I held a variety of roles within Training, Leadership Development, and Human Resources. I worked in industries ranging from healthcare to high-tech to national restaurant chains. I steadily climbed the corporate ladder, made lots of money, and got lots of bonuses, promotions, and recognition. For most of my career, I was a good "corporate player." I learned how to be successful, how to get along with challenging bosses, and how to be politically savvy. I remember feeling pride at knowing how to succeed in the corporate system. At one point, while working for a company I truly loved, a good friend of mine said "You always did drink the Kool-Aid, didn't you?" I could clearly see it was not easy for some, and in private, even I got jaded sometimes. I usually came around though, landing a new role, getting a new boss, or just finding a new reservoir of motivation.

However, later in my career, it got harder and harder to find that motivation. For one, I was getting older. In my mid-40s, I began to question where I was going, wondering to myself—*is this all there is?* When I looked at the more senior executives, some of whom were my friends and mentors, I wasn't sure I wanted their lifestyle, with the stress and long hours. To me, it didn't look like there was a reward at the top of the ladder beyond just a bigger paycheck, and I wondered whether the bigger paycheck was worth it. I'd begun to feel that climbing the corporate ladder and playing the corporate game was like selling my soul.

The other thing going on was that I found myself in a situation worse than any I'd been in before. The first half of my corporate career had been during boom times, including working for a Silicon Valley great during the height of the dot-com boom. But the latter half was a consistent stream of reorganizations, layoffs, and poor business results. That by itself was not the issue. I was always the first to say that as a student of leadership and

organizational behavior, I learned more under those difficult business circumstances than I ever could have during
boom times. But the constant churn of changing strategies
and organizational restructurings sapped my energy. And
that's when I got the boss from hell.

Back to Monday morning. As I stand ready to walk into
her office, it feels like it's all come to a head. For the first
time in my career, I think it's possible I could get fired. I
realize in that moment that for my entire career, there has
always been a fear under the surface of getting fired, even
if I never explicitly acknowledged it. This fear has a lot of
cousins that might be easier to recognize, such as fear of
being criticized, fear of a bad performance review, or fear
of simply looking bad. As I walk into her office, the
anxiety settles and I feel calm and clear. Whatever is to
come, I will survive it.

She doesn't fire me. It's clear she can't fire me, because
I haven't given her any legitimate reason, and I still have
supporters at the top of the organization more senior to
her. But I haven't been an easy employee for her. We've
clashed on style and in substance, causing my motivation
to plummet, and everything she tried to make it better
only made it worse for me. One thing is clear in this
meeting however: she wants me out. The feeling is mutual,
of course. She offers me a choice, an opportunity to

depart on my own terms, and 24 hours later, I take the offer.

———————

That day in my boss's office seems like ages ago as I write this. But it was an important turning point in my adult working life. It was simultaneously terrifying and liberating. It was terrifying because I was in the prime years of my career. I was 44 years old, with a big mortgage, a young family depending on my income, and I had no idea how I was going to create the change I was looking for. On the other hand, it was liberating. I didn't make the decision with the intention of just finding another job. I decided it was time to make a serious change in my career.

While before I had the feeling that my path would take me through to retirement, I was now looking forward with the belief that just about anything was possible. I was starting fresh. I was taking a leap, with no guarantee that I would land on my feet, and *I felt alive!* Since I took that leap, I have grown more as a professional and as a person than any other time aside from the beginning of my career.

Fairly quickly, I began working toward getting my coaching credentials. My first exposure to coaching was in 1995, and by 2000 I had begun incorporating it into the work I did with company leaders. I always imagined that one day I would start my own practice and do it for a living.

A few months into my new journey, I had an idea while working with a colleague who was coaching me. As difficult as my final year inside the corporate world was, a few months' distance was giving me perspective, and I began to feel a sense of purpose again. Twenty years earlier, I had left graduate school with the idea to make the corporate world great. Now, that same purpose returned, albeit with a lot more personal experience baked into it. In that coaching session with my colleague, I irreverently declared my new professional purpose was to **liberate Corporate America from hell**.

At first, I felt like I shouldn't say that out loud. Twenty years of corporate conditioning had me worried about how I might be perceived. I wanted to make my living coaching within the corporate world, and if I told people I thought corporate life was hell, I might lose my credibility. So I kept it close to the vest, sharing it only in private. Then a funny thing happened. Every time I shared this idea, I would get a knowing laugh or a nod of recognition that corporate life did indeed need some liberation. People got it. Anyone who had spent enough time working inside the corporate world knew exactly what I was talking about.

It's no surprise really. The Gallup organization has been measuring employee engagement in the corporate world for years, and they've consistently found that about

70% of employees are not engaged with their job (or worse, are "actively disengaged"). Another way to think about this is that they don't feel positively motivated. It seems I wasn't alone in my feelings on the corporate world.

As I continued to gain perspective in the first couple years of my post-corporate journey, I began to understand one idea more clearly. I understood that Corporate Hell was the result of failures in leadership. I'd known this for some time, but now that I had more time to reflect on it, my understanding deepened. It's pretty obvious when you look at it that poor leadership is all around you in many corporate settings. It's easy to point to all those leadership failures around you and place blame for why your life is miserable. At my lowest point, I could have regaled you with stories of my horrible boss or described the many ways that I felt top management was making bad decisions. Or maybe I would have complained about individuals on my team and how they just weren't stepping up like I thought they should. All of those things might have had some truth in them, but none of them are the failures I'm talking about.

I realized that in the end, there is only one leader I can point to. I don't control my boss, or any of the other people around me. I can only control one person, and that person is me. When I truly let that sink in, when I truly understood it, deep down, it became clear to me why I was unhappy.

I was failing as a leader.

A well-meaning friend might tell me "C'mon Mike, you're not failing. No one's perfect. You're taking too much accountability and letting others off the hook." Let me be clear. I do not mean to excuse poor leadership behavior in others. But what I do know is that every time I blame another person for my own unhappiness, I am failing as a leader. I don't control other people, but I do control my response to other people and my response to everything that happens to me. Many people buy into this idea intellectually. Far fewer actually reach an experiential understanding of it. It is one of the principal aims of this book to show you how you can be one of those people.

Is this book right for you?

When I say "Corporate Life Is Hell," I'm referring to an *inner experience*. The term resonates with people because they've experienced it, but whether they realize it or not, the experience originates on the inside. It's a state of mind. We're not unhappy because of the way other people treat us; we're unhappy because of *how we respond* to the treatment we get from other people.

As such, it's possible that this book won't be quite what you were expecting when you saw the title. But what I mean by saying "Corporate Life Is Hell" is that there are many characteristics of life in the corporate world that can lead us to feel unhappy. If you're hoping this book will expose everything that's wrong with the corporate world, then you may be disappointed. Certainly, there are a myriad of things in corporate life that are worthy of criticism. I'm sure you could tell me stories. I've heard the stories and I've lived my own stories.

However, what this book concerns is the *effect* those things can have on you, and more importantly, how you can *change* that effect. This means you have to be introspective on this journey. If you don't have much interest in examining your own inner experience (i.e., what's going on in your own head), then this book might not be for you. On the other hand, if you have an open mind, and are willing to take a look inward as you read, the results can be life-changing.

There are two more points on the question of whether this book is right for you, and they are implied in the subtitle: *How to Liberate the Leader Within You and Be Happy in Your Career.* The implication of the first part is that you have a leader within you. Another way to think of this is that **You Are a Leader**. If you're wondering whether that applies to you, let me be clear from the outset. You do not need to be a corporate executive or even have a senior level position in the organization to benefit from the ideas expressed in this book. In fact, it's a central premise of the book that one can lead from any position in the organization. While it's been my experience that "Corporate Hell" grows the higher you get in the corporate management hierarchy—you don't need to be a senior executive to experience it. More importantly, you don't need to be an executive to do anything about it. That being said, senior executives tend to leave a bigger footprint with their actions, which means they have a bigger ability to make life hell for others. Because of that, I believe that senior executives need this book as much as anyone, but it applies at any level.

The second half of the subtitle goes a bit deeper. To *Be Happy in Your Career* might sound like a very big promise. It is big. In fact, it's bigger than your career. It's difficult to be truly happy in your career if you're not really happy in life. That's how big I'm aiming. What this book will cover is no less than a formula for happiness in life. I don't mean fleeting pleasure, or worldly success here. What I mean is a deeper feeling of peace and contentedness in your life. It's the opposite of hell. In this book, I dive into some deep topics from psychology to philosophy to ancient spirituality. If that sounds interesting to you, read on. If it makes you feel apprehensive, that's okay, open your mind—and your heart—and give it a shot. If it sounds boring or horrible, then put the book down now and pick it up again someday when you feel ready.

How is this book organized?

This book is about leadership. The context in which I'm writing about leadership is the corporate world, but in the bigger picture, leadership can show up anywhere, in how you lead your life, how you lead yourself, and how you lead others, such as in a corporate team.

The definition I use for leadership is the choice to **take responsibility** for one's world. Leaders take responsibility for their world, or more accurately, they take responsibility for *the impact* they have on the world. A leader's world starts on the inside, in the mind and in the heart, and it expands outward from there, to other people and the world at large. To develop as a leader is to expand the scope of the world you seek to impact, but it always starts with *you*.

Taking responsibility begins with a desire for something to be different, anything from how you're feeling inside to solving world hunger, and it includes taking action to bring that change into being.

Before you can take responsibility for your world, you need to **connect** with it. You can't take responsibility for changing something that you don't have an intimate connection with. You can't mold the clay unless you lay your hands on it. You can't inspire other human beings unless you connect with them. You can't change your own feelings and response to what the world gives you unless you connect with yourself deep inside.

Even before you connect, you need to **show up** in a particular way. Yes, obviously you need to show up physically, but *how* you show up, including mentally and emotionally, affects your ability to connect, which in turn powers the impact you have when you take responsibility.

Show up, connect, and take responsibility

In Part 1 of this book, we'll explore how you **show up** as a leader, with courage, purpose, and authenticity.

- Chapter 1 explores the way that **everyone is a leader**, no matter what your job position, no matter how sophisticated your skills. The big question is whether you choose to lead, which requires courage.
- Chapter 2 encourages you to **decide why you're here**, tapping into the power of purpose, and whether you're living and working "on purpose."
- Chapter 3 will take you deeper, asking you to consider how you allow yourself to be seen by others. You'll **take off the mask** and examine what it means to be authentic.

In Part 2, we'll explore what it means to **connect**, non-judgmentally, with yourself and with other people, and see how doing so empowers you.

- Chapter 4 reminds you that you are leading human beings. You'll learn to **lead people, manage things**, which means that you must approach leadership not as a means to an end, but as a human relationship.

- Chapter 5 challenges you to **be present** to the world around you and the people within it. Doing so will give you presence, which is what most great leaders have.
- Chapter 6 introduces you to your Inner Judge, who is a big source of disconnection between people. To reconnect, you'll need to **tear down the wall** that is between you and the people you lead.

In Part 3, you'll **take responsibility** as we broaden the perspective and put your leadership to good use to create change in your world.

- Chapter 7 starts with a paradox—in order to create change, you must first **accept what is**.
- Chapter 8 focuses your attention to stop complaining about Corporate Hell and **create change** in your world.
- Chapter 9 will leave you with the choice to be and to act differently, in order to **liberate yourself** from Corporate Hell.

PART I

SHOW UP

Leadership development always begins on the inside. People will choose to follow you because of who you are, more than what you say and do. They might decide who they think you are based on what you say and do, but it's their belief in who you are that matters. This means that if you truly want to have influence in this world, you must first work on yourself. You have to show up—with courage, purpose, and authenticity.

1

BE A LEADER

Courage is being scared to death… and saddling up anyway.

— JOHN WAYNE

My high school English teacher Mr. Allen once told me I was a natural leader, and for the next several years, the thought kept popping into my head: *"Really? How does he know that? What does that even mean?"* I wasn't the captain of the football team; I mostly warmed the bench. I wasn't class president; I wasn't even involved or interested in student government. I wasn't in charge of any clubs and I wasn't the guy organizing the school dance (thank God). I thought, if I'm such a natural leader, how come I'm not in charge of stuff?

A few years later, right after college, I took a two-month backpacking trip through Europe. I went on the trip alone, but not a single day went by when I wasn't traveling and hanging out with other backpackers I met along the way. An event that happened one evening on the Italian Riviera stands out in my mind.

I had been traveling along the French and Italian Riviera for several days and had been meeting lots of small groups of people. I was in the Cinque Terre at a big youth hostel called Mama Rosa's, and many of the same people I'd met were also staying there. During a long day of hiking, sightseeing, swimming in the sea, and doing touristy stuff, I kept mentioning to people that we should meet up for dinner that evening. I could sense that I was getting some traction, but it still surprised me when about 20 people gathered that evening to head out together, and they were all looking to *me* for the plan! They were mostly in smaller groups that didn't know each other, and I was the glue that was holding everyone together.

In that moment, it hit me, this must be what Mr. Allen meant. For some reason, these people have decided to follow me tonight. My "plan" was to buy a bunch of bottles of wine, some bread and cheese, and go watch the sunset together. Sitting on these big rocks jutting out into the Mediterranean Sea, with a group of 20 new friends I didn't even know a few days earlier, I was about as happy as I could be. I was aware that I had created this little shindig by the sea—simply by leading the way.

Leadership is an active choice

Although we usually use the word "leadership" to mean a position, leadership is not a position. It does not depend on hierarchical authority and it should not be equated with being in charge or being the boss. We often put leaders in charge of stuff, because that's where we need leadership, but the actual act of leadership, the "way of being" of leadership, is independent of one's job. Everyone is a leader, or at least, everyone has within them the potential to be a leader, regardless of their position in life or on the organizational chart.

Leadership is a choice to take responsibility for something in your world, no matter how small, no matter how big. If you're walking through the city with friends, and you speak up to say you know a shortcut to your destination, you've just committed a leadership act. If you're tired of your neighbor's dog barking all night and you knock on their door to address it, you've chosen to take responsibility, rather than sit home and complain. If you are the CEO of a multinational firm and you empower your front-line employees to make their own decisions, you are leading. If you work at the front counter of a casual restaurant and you listen to a dissatisfied customer and then eagerly do what you can to fix it, you are leading.

We are confronted regularly with situations that we would like to be different. You wish something would stop.

You wish something would start. You believe the world needs more of something, or less of something. You want to feel different. You want to be different. You have a desire for something to be different in your world, and whether you realize it or not, you are faced with a choice. Will you do something about it, or will you just tolerate the way things are? Will you speak up? Will you take some action? Will you shift your perspective on the situation? The choice you face is whether you will take responsibility in some way for that thing you want to be different.

I'm talking about a binary state of being. You've either made a choice to be responsible, or you haven't. Often, that leadership choice shows up in action, but it also can show up in choosing a "way of being," such as being patient, or kind, or even angry if the situation warrants it. Create and follow an intention to change something—and you are leading. Ignore that intention, even if deep down you believe there is a better way—and you are failing to lead. Fundamentally, you have this choice every moment of your life.

What's holding you back?

Actively choosing your response is at the root of leadership. However, this is not always as easy as it sounds. To explain what I mean, let's take a moment to look at the neurophysiology of your brain. It is a fundamental characteristic of your brain to *approach or avoid*. Millions of years of evolution have created a brain that is exceptionally good at approaching rewards and avoiding risks. This is enormously useful when you're a member of a hunter-gatherer tribe making your way in the world. It helps to pursue the things that help you thrive (nutritious food, safe shelter, sex) and avoid the things that kill you (saber-toothed tigers and poisonous mushrooms). Today, we face relatively few physical threats in our environment. Even the ones you might think of—crime, terrorism, accidents—are not really immediate physical threats. The idea that we might become the victim of such threats creates a fear in our mind, and our body treats that threat the same as an immediate physical threat. That's the root of our stress response, but that's a topic for another book. My point is that we actually spend a fairly large portion of our lives responding to threats that only exist—in the immediate sense—in our minds. We act from fear.

It wasn't until my mid-40s that I truly admitted to myself how much of my life I was living out of fear. But what was I afraid of? Maybe looking bad, making a mistake, failing, getting rejected, getting taken advantage of, being treated unfairly, being told what to do, getting my feelings hurt, getting in a fight, getting fired, getting embarrassed, losing money. I could go on. From the outside, you wouldn't have guessed this, because those fears didn't necessarily stop me from taking risks, growing as a person, and moving forward in life. But it's hard to exaggerate how much those fears may have held me back from what was possible.

When you're experiencing these types of fear, it feels like you're the only one feeling them. The truth is that these fears are ubiquitous. Yes, some people are better than others at hiding them. Some people feel them more (or less) than other people. But neuroscience tells us that these fears are a natural part of the brain. They may have evolved in a world where survival depended on them, but today, they exist in a world where the threats we face are almost all social in nature, i.e., they are triggered by our interactions with other people. Over the past twenty years or so, the field of neuroscience has made tremendous progress in identifying and categorizing the ways in which our brains feel threatened in social situations. In his book *Your Brain at Work*, David Rock summarizes five of these situations, using the acronym SCARF to represent them. It's not difficult to see how the corporate world is a fertile ground for all five of these dynamics to create a threat response:

- **Status** is about one's relative standing compared to others. Common threat triggers in the corporate world might include performance rankings, the organization chart, and office space planning.
- **Certainty** represents the brain's need to

eliminate uncertainty. Common threat triggers include corporate reorganizations, mergers and acquisitions, unclear goals, and lack of company vision.

- **Autonomy** is the desire to control our own destiny. Common threat triggers include autocratic bosses, rigid processes, and stifling corporate cultures.
- **Relatedness** is the need to feel we are part of the group. Common threat triggers include being left out of a project, failing to have one's contributions recognized, or being criticized publicly by your boss.
- **Fairness** is simply the need to feel treated fairly. Common threat triggers include compensation practices, subjective performance evaluations, and corporate politics.

In other words, the corporate world is full of situations where your brain may feel under threat. None of these situations represent a real physical threat, yet our body responds in the same way that it does to a physical threat —and that response can hold you back from being a leader. We all experience fear, but fear need only control our behavior to the degree that *we let it*. Remember, you have the choice in how to respond.

Choose love, not fear

You can make your choice from a place of fear, or you can choose the opposite. What is the opposite of fear? It's love. The fear response is fight or flight. The love response is embrace and engage. If you encounter a saber-toothed tiger, I don't recommend embrace and engage, but for just about every fear I detailed in the last section, you have this choice available to you.

What I'm talking about is **_leadership engagement_**. You can engage your inner leader at any time, in any situation. Or you can disengage. You decide.

Life happens. Your whole life is a steady stream of moments, every one of which presents you with an opportunity to choose to respond from love or from fear. You can't choose what feelings arise in you, but you can choose how you respond to those feelings. When fear arises, you can choose courage. Having courage doesn't mean being unafraid. In fact, courage cannot exist without fear. The goal is not to never be afraid. The goal is to act courageously and face your fears with love in your heart. Be courageous and be a leader.

The title of this book implies a negative atmosphere in the corporate world. Corporate life, like life in general, just is what it is. Whether it's positive or negative, fun or boring, miserable or blissful is all a function of perspective and how we engage with it. It's just a situation. Corporate

Hell, as I'm using the phrase, is a subjective experience, not an objective reality. How we experience it is largely dependent upon how we respond to it. Consciously choosing to respond *as a leader* is the first step toward liberation.

Everyone's a leader

"But I can't," you say. "I'm not in a position to make a difference. It doesn't matter what I want; my boss makes the decisions. I don't have the power."

It's a myth that you can only be a leader under the right circumstances. Leadership is not a position. It does not depend on hierarchical authority and it should not be equated with being in charge or being the boss. It is true that some positions offer a bigger platform for leadership, but in no way should that stop you from leading, regardless of position or ranking in a hierarchy.

Much of the confusion comes from the idea that leaders need to be at the top or out in front in order to lead. It's the classic view of leadership that encompasses having a vision, setting the direction, and getting everyone from here to there. Unfortunately, that view of leadership is severely limited. One of the biggest failures of leadership is the failure to get out of the way, to sit down and listen, and to let other people take the reins when it's time. That directive from-the-front mode of leadership is frequently necessary, but it's one-dimensional. Effective leadership needs to be multi-dimensional, which is good news in the idea that everyone is a leader. If leadership can be exercised from all angles, then leadership is not limited just to those at the top of the org chart, or the ones setting the pace out front.

In their book *Co-Active Leadership*, Karen and Henry Kimsey-House define five ways to lead, each corresponding to a different perspective or dimension of leadership. At the center of their model is the ***Leader Within***. From this perspective, one is taking responsibility for one's self and life. Part 1 of this book is all about leading from within.

Another dimension is ***Leader in Front***, which is the dimension most people are familiar with. Leading from the front is important, but it must be more than just moving people from here to there. Leaders in front take a stand for their vision and then rally people around it. They create an atmosphere of courage and safety for others, and most importantly, they know when to step back and support the leadership of others.

The next dimension is ***Leader Behind***. This is the choice to point one's energy toward the success of others. As a Leadership Coach, I am most often a Leader Behind, supporting my clients in what they seek to create in their world. The executive who empowers their staff, supports them with coaching, and champions their causes is a

Leader Behind. The assistant who enthusiastically devotes their energy to their boss's effectiveness and efficiency is also a Leader Behind.

A **Leader Beside** is one who knows how to partner and share the spotlight with another person. I see leaders fail all the time because they struggle to share leadership with their peers. Leaders Beside are capable of *designing relationships* with each other to serve a role where two can do better than one.

The final dimension is **Leader in the Field**. In each of the previous parts of the model, the leader's attention is focused in a specific direction: within, in front, behind, and beside. A Leader in the Field has their attention focused on the energetic field all around them. It's not a laser focus on individual people or projects. It's a softer focus on the environment, the collective people within it, and the energy passing among them. For me, this is about presence. It's about being present in what's happening, in the moment, and intuitively giving voice to what you see. We'll talk more about this in Chapter 5. If it's possible to lead from any of these dimensions, then leadership is not dependent on any set of external circumstances. You can lead from wherever you are.

Engage your inner leader

This is where liberating the leader within you starts. You

have to first recognize that you are a leader, regardless of your outward situation. Make the choice to lead and expand your view of leadership beyond just being in charge. In a crisis, leading from the front may be what's needed, but when it's the only dimension being embodied, it creates negative consequences. The biggest consequence is that it eventually creates disconnection and separation—mental, emotional, even physical—from those who the leader seeks to lead. Almost inevitably, if you try to lead exclusively by being the boss, you will eventually make life hell for yourself and for others.

In every moment, in every situation, ask yourself what's needed. Knowing what's needed depends on several factors, including being present enough to notice. However, this is hard if you don't know what you actually want. Clarifying what you want, why you want it, and how to articulate it are therefore the subjects of our next chapter.

Chapter summary

- Leadership is not a position. It's an active choice to take responsibility for your world.
- Your world begins inside of you, in your heart

and mind, and expands outward from there—
to your behavior, to other people, and to the
world at large. Developing as a leader means
increasing the scope of what you take
responsibility for in the world.

- Fear is what holds you back from taking
  responsibility. Your brain was shaped by
  evolution to have a keen sense of fear about
  threats in the world. In the modern world,
  those threats are mostly social in nature, but
  your brain doesn't make that distinction, and
  this fear stops you from taking responsibility
  when and where you can.

- The alternative to fear is love. Approaching
  life's challenges with love, rather than shrinking
  from them in fear, is leadership engagement.
  It's the choice of love over fear.

- Everyone has the potential to lead, from
  wherever they are, and in whatever
  circumstance they find themselves. One does
  not have to "be in charge" to lead.

Coach's assignment

- Engage your inner leader.
- Reflect on this question: where in your life are

you sitting back while your instincts are telling you to step forward?

- Actively choose one thing you think someone should do something about—and be the one who does something about it.

2

DECIDE WHY YOU'RE HERE

The mystery of human existence lies not in just staying alive, but in finding something to live for.

— FYODOR DOSTOYEVSKY

A few years ago, I was participating in a leadership development retreat in the Great Smoky Mountains of North Carolina. Each morning, we participated in the same rituals, which included physical, spiritual, and mindfulness exercises, partly as a group and partly on our own. On one particular morning, I had an experience that still resonates powerfully within me to this day. After the group exercise, I was walking silently and alone. I took each step deliberately and slowly. The setting was a small farm in a rugged little valley, with a stream running through it, joining a larger river further off. It was a beautiful, crisp morning, with the sun shining, and I was quite literally communing with nature. At one point, I paused and squatted down to look at the ground and discovered that each blade of grass was coated with a layer of frost. I could see the detail in the frost, as though they were giant ice crystals. I began moving again and approached a healthy-looking tree with big, broad leaves. I came up close enough to see the veins in the leaves and was certain I could feel the life force emanating from this great silent being. From there, I moved again until I found an overgrown trail down a slope to a small clearing by the flowing stream. I stood and watched the water for some time before I began to slowly drop some dead leaves and twigs into the water, watching them drift downstream, following the natural path around rocks and through eddies. Something about the idea of the dead twigs triggered a voice in my head that said "I am alive." The voice repeated itself several times before it settled down again.

I then began to recall the people in my life who were no longer alive, and the voice said their names in my head. The kid I played soccer with who was killed in a tragic accident in his home when we were just 10 years old. My childhood friend and neighbor who was killed in a car accident my sophomore year in college. My friend from junior high, who in his late 20s committed suicide. All four of my grandparents. And my father-in-law, who lost his battle with cancer.

Soon I was walking again, back toward the retreat center, and again the voice in my head began reminding me I am alive. *I am alive.* My pace was faster now, and I could feel my lungs, my muscles, and my entire being becoming more energized. Breathing heavily, walking briskly, still feeling *I am alive.* Then a wave of emotion came over me and I could feel tears on my face. *I am alive.*

The last hundred yards back to the retreat center was an uphill trail through a dense forest. Huffing up the trail, legs pumping, head down, the voice was still repeating in my head, *I AM ALIVE, I AM ALIVE*, with ever more urgency, until I rounded a corner, and very suddenly, there was a break in the trees, and I felt the bright sunlight broadside me. The sensation was like a hand reaching out and grabbing me by the shoulder, stopping me in my tracks and turning me to face the sun. I stood there, eyes closed, face pointed to the sky, feeling the sun's warmth on my face. The entire world went silent, save for the distant gurgle of the stream, the sounds of life in the forest, and my heartbeat pounding in my chest. For several moments I stood there, breathing, smiling. Then I made my way back to the retreat center, sat down quietly, and began to write in my journal.

Meaning of life

I am not a traditionally religious person and I don't tell this story to imply that I spoke to God. It was an experience, deeply felt, that moved me. It had such an impact on me because it got right to the heart of the question: what is the meaning of life?

What is the meaning of life? The nature of the question is misleading, and if I adjust it slightly, it opens up more possibilities. Try this one instead: what is the meaning of *your* life? Instead of looking for a meaning of life somewhere out there, what if the meaning of your life is whatever you make of it? You decide the meaning of your life. When your brief time in this human form is complete, what will you have made of it? What impact will you have created in the world? Whose lives will you have touched? In what way will you have transformed yourself over the course of your life?

I know this much: one thing that can make life hell is feeling that it has no meaning. The same is true at the level of your career and the work that you do. Some of the times I felt most acutely unhappy with the corporate life were those times when it felt like what I was doing didn't matter. It happened more often than you might expect. Whether through organizational incompetence, flawed decision-making, or simply my own disagreement with the company's choices, that feeling of spinning my wheels while getting nowhere was a central component of Corporate Hell. At the level of your life, it can be soul-draining.

Another way to rephrase the question is to ask what is the *purpose* of your life? Viktor Frankl's answer to this question was that it is to create meaning in one's life. In 1944, he was sent to Auschwitz by the Nazis. In a place where one can be forgiven for giving up all hope for life, Frankl discovered that this freedom to create meaning in one's life is the one thing no one could ever take from him. Indeed, it's what sustained him and gave him the strength to endure unimaginable atrocities. After the war, Viktor Frankl wrote the book *Man's Search for Meaning*, in which he defined the "will to create meaning" as the primary motivating force in life.

Corporate life is no concentration camp, nor is your own life, but that doesn't make it any less important to create meaning in your life. If anything, modern life, and corporate life in particular, with all its perks and luxuries, can lure you into forgetting what's most meaningful. Think about the large company who loses sight of their original purpose in the world and starts thinking their main purpose is simply to make money. Or the person who loses sight of what matters in life and thinks that making money and acquiring things is the key to happiness. Both run into trouble eventually.

One of the surest routes to Corporate Hell is feeling like the work you do is meaningless. I believe it's the duty of a corporate executive to instill a sense of purpose and meaning in the work being done by the organization. In practice, that doesn't always happen, but that doesn't mean you can't figure it out for yourself. Meaning and purpose are at the heart of a fulfilled corporate life, so finding your own sense of purpose in the work you do simply requires following your heart.

Follow your heart to find your values

Most people have a tendency to think that if they do what's expected of them in life, then success and happiness will follow. This is a logical way of thinking. If I meet the world's expectations of me, the world will deliver what I want from life. Unfortunately, nothing could be further from the truth. The world will just keep delivering you the same expectations, albeit at an increasing rate of expectancy. The more you meet expectations, the more is expected of you in the same pattern.

You want life happiness, so you do what you're supposed to do, expecting that happiness will ensue. Study hard. Get a good job. Work hard and climb the ladder. Your reward is continued expectations to study hard, get the next promotion, work even harder, and climb higher. There is no reward at the end of this path because it's not leading toward what you want. It's leading toward what's expected of you, and while logic told you if you played by the rules you would end up happy—it wasn't true.

Your head is not where you find what you want. You might be accurately storing the idea in your head of what you want, but that's not where you found it in the first place. You've always known what you want by following your heart. Your head gets in the way, with its fear-driven objections about what will happen if you follow your heart. So you compromise on your deeper wants.

The best way to think about what you really want is in terms of *values*. You want what you value. What you value often gets obscured, even to yourself. It gets obscured by focusing on what's expected of you by others. It gets obscured by time and repetition. You slip into behavioral patterns and forget to remind yourself of what you truly value. You lose focus on what you value until it becomes obscured. For this reason, it's imperative that you occasionally clarify your values for yourself.

Excavating your values

The simplest way to do this is to ask yourself, *what do I value?* and then write down your own reply. It's a good start, but if your values are not in focus, then the direct approach often won't reveal much. Instead, you need to get creative with your questions. Ask yourself, *what would you do if you won enough money to be financially independent for the rest of your life?* If your first answer is quit my job and go lie on the beach, then ask yourself what you would do when you eventually got bored with that.

Go deeper. Imagine you have been offered the job as CEO of a company whose business perfectly matches what you want to offer to the world.

- What would your company create into existence?
- How would you lead that company?
- What would guide your decisions about whom to hire?
- How would you market your product to the world?
- What choices would you make in your strategy?

Or get even more imaginative. You are the commander of a colonization expedition to a distant planet. The planet is perfectly suited for human habitation and you are bringing with you everything and everyone you need to begin a new society.

- What choices would you make in building this society?
- How would people be involved in the governing of the society?
- What would commerce look like?
- How would people work together, and entertain themselves?

You can make up your own questions. The idea is to make up as many as you need, getting as imaginative as you can.

- What job would you do if money was not a requirement and you knew you could move on whenever you're ready? And most importantly, why?
- If you inherited a billion-dollar charity foundation, what cause would you champion and why?

As you ask yourself the questions, write down your answers in a stream of consciousness fashion. When you feel like you have enough words on paper, read what you've written back to yourself and reflect upon it. Then take these steps:

1. Circle the important words, especially the ones that tend to repeat themselves.
2. Start drawing lines that connect common words and ideas.
3. Identify particular clusters of ideas and pull them out.
4. Sort the clusters of ideas into a grouping of no less than three and no more than about six or seven.

This is the beginning of excavating your values. I call it "values excavation" because your values already exist, resulting from your life experience up to this moment. You are not creating your values—*you are uncovering them*. What you value is reflected in the choices you make, and the questions are intended to bring your choices to the surface. It's tricky, because you may not currently be living your life in alignment with your values, which is why the creative and hypothetical questions are so important. Later in this chapter we'll talk about living in alignment with your values, but for now, start excavating.

With your grouping of three to seven clusters of ideas, the last step is to label your values. Give each cluster a **label**, plus an **emotional word picture**. The label should be a word or phrase that represents the ideas in the cluster. The emotional word picture should be some kind of mental image or phrase that is personal to you, and that evokes the richness, depth, and specificity of the value. It only has to make sense for you, so don't worry about making it acceptable for others.

For example, I might have a cluster of ideas around telling the truth, even when it's unpopular, and being honest in all my relationships. The mistake would be using the generic label "Integrity." There's nothing wrong with valuing integrity, but as a useful tool it falls short. Who doesn't value integrity? And what do you mean by it, exactly, compared to the next person I ask, and the next person after that? You want a bit more descriptive label for yourself, like maybe "Relentless Truth-telling," or "Extreme Honesty," or "Constructive Observation." See how each of those labels brings up a different flavor of integrity? Make your labels more descriptive of what you truly value.

The emotional word picture can be anything that evokes the value, such as a person (real or fictitious), a place, an object, a behavior, or an idea. It doesn't need to be descriptive; it just has to *evoke the value for you personally*. Maybe for integrity, you choose your father's name, because he lived his life that way and you learned that value from him.

To give you an example of this (and to let myself be seen by you, here and now), I've listed my own values here.

Liberated Leadership
Living a life of purpose, unconstrained by my own fears. Being fully and authentically "self-expressed," in service to my life's purpose. Creating change to make the world a better place.
"Maximus"

Intimate Connection
Love and compassion for my fellow humans. Family bonds. Creating appropriate intimacy and vulnerability in my relationships, and in all parts of my life. Risking rejection for the sake of connection.
"My Open Heart"

Integral Truth

Scientific truth. Accuracy. Competence. Knowledge and Education. All of this, from a holistic—not just reductionist—perspective. The integrity of the whole, in addition to the knowledge of the parts.

"Carl Sagan"

Inner Peace

Natural beauty, inside and out. The experience of spaciousness, expansiveness, solitude, and a quiet mind.

"Yosemite Valley"

Courageous Adventure

Overcoming fears, getting uncomfortable, stretching myself. Finding joy in anything I do.

"Traveling the World"

Spiritual Meaning

Inspiration. Breathing life into my own spirit. Experiencing all aspects of life as a unique expression of the Universe. Transcending limited belief systems to arrive at a deeper appreciation of the meaning of life.

"Universal Consciousness"

Harmonious Being

Going with the flow of life, rather than resisting its currents. Letting go of control. Overcoming ego. Non-attachment, non-resistance.

"The Way"

I'm not a fan of the way in which many companies and consultants do values clarification today, which is to provide a list of value labels and have their staff sort through them, winnowing and narrowing until each person has a list of values. What makes this process less than ideal in my mind is that the original source was a generic deck of cards, rather than the person's own internal spirit, and the end result fails to connect with a deeper meaning. I want to yawn when people tell me that their values are integrity, customer service, and fun! There's nothing wrong with those ideals—it's just that they are too generic to carry any personal meaning.

So start by excavating with questions. Explore your own answers, and creatively describe what you discover. Then keep your creatively labeled values handy so you can refer to them often, comparing the life you're living to what you know you value. Understanding your personal values in life will help you understand whether or not you're honoring those values in the work that you do and the career that you've chosen. It will help you transcend Corporate Hell.

Live and work on purpose

Why do you do the work that you do? How did you get into it? At your most idealistic, what impact do you imagine you are making with your work?

It's likely that part of your answer is to make money so

you can live the life you want to live. In that case, the second part becomes crucial. Working solely to make money—without any larger sense of purpose in your life —is a near-certain recipe for unhappiness. For that reason, before you even answer the question of *why do you do the work that you do?*, it's helpful to answer the question, *why do I exist on earth, at this moment?*

Articulating your life's purpose

You are a unique expression of the Universe. Regardless of your spiritual beliefs, it's not difficult to see there is no one else exactly like you on this earth. (I'll explain this a little more in Chapter 5). So what will you make of your life?

Imagine you are attending your own 90th birthday party. The party has been planned by someone very close to you, and they've invited every important person in your life. They have all arrived, ready to celebrate you tonight. One by one, they stand at the podium and say a few words about you and your life. Ask yourself now:

- What are they saying?
- What impact have you made on them?
- What impact have you made on the world?
- In what small ways is the world different because you've been in it?
- Whose lives have you affected?

A recent book that had a big impact on me is Bronnie Ware's *The Top Five Regrets of the Dying: A Life Transformed by the Dearly Departing.* Ms. Ware spent several years caring for people in their final years, and was fortunate to gain their wisdom about life. She discovered that what people regret in their final years has little to do with what they accomplished in terms of worldly success, and more to do with how they engaged with the world and the people around them.

What will matter to you on your deathbed? How long we each get in this form on earth is unknown. What you do with your time is up to you. You've probably heard it said that no one looks back on life from their deathbed and wishes they'd spent more time in the office. That is certainly true for me, but it's also true that I want to look back from my deathbed and see that the work I did was in service of the larger purpose I felt in my life. I want my own life's purpose to be at the heart of the corporate life that I led.

Write your own life purpose statement

The best way to clarify your own life's purpose is to write it down. It doesn't have to be perfect, overwhelming, or profound. It just has to be expressed. Once you do it, it becomes a living statement, evolving with you as you grow, so it's not critical to get it perfect. It is critical to write it down.

I guide my clients through this process by visualizing situations like the 90th birthday party example, capturing their answers to questions posed, and (similar to the values excavation described earlier) sorting and combining them to find common themes. The goal is to harness those common themes into a two-part statement:

- The first half of the statement completes the phrase "I am…" with some kind of metaphor that captures the essence of _who you are_ when fully expressed in your natural way.
- The second part of the statement captures the metaphorical essence of what you are _meant to do_ while on this earth.

Put together, these statements might sound something like this: _"I am the mountain guide, leading people to the comfort and warmth of the campfire,"_ or _"I am the link in the chain who connects knowledge across generations,"_ or _"I am a passionate sun that illuminates, impacts, and grows ideas and people to greatness."_

The two halves of the statement represent the **being** and the **doing** of your life's purpose. A life of doing—without any sense of who you are—is just as incomplete as a life of being, with no action taken to make a real impact in and on the world. They are metaphors to represent, in very few words, something much deeper inside of you. Your purpose statement needs to evoke what's deep within you, not be a marketing-ready statement for others.

Put your purpose to work

Once you know why you're here, on earth, at this moment, you can more readily make the connection to why you do the work you do, why you spend your time the way you do, whom you associate with, and so on. Everything you do in life and who you are in life is an expression of your life's purpose. You can now answer the question, are you living life on purpose? The more *on purpose* you are, the more resonance you will feel in the work you do. The more off purpose you are, the more you'll feel dissonance and the more you'll feel like you're in Corporate Hell.

When I quit my last internal corporate job, I was feeling dissonance for a variety of reasons. At the time, I was the head of People Development for a major organization, responsible for the professional development of several thousand people. But I didn't feel like I was developing anyone. I was running all the processes, pulling the levers, turning the dials, making cases to senior management about what they should be doing, but I didn't feel like I was developing anyone. In fact, I came to discover that these corporate processes were not only poor at actually developing people, but in some cases, they were working against people's ability to develop themselves. It was this feeling, maybe more than all the others, that finally led me to make a change in my career. The work I do today is a more direct and powerful expression of my life's purpose.

So decide why you're here. Decide why you're on this earth, and then connect that to why you show up for work every morning. It's possible that this process will lead you to make a change in the work you do, but there is no reason to assume that must be the case. It could be making changes in where you put your focus. It could be shifting your own perspective about the work you're doing. All that matters is that *you* are the one doing the choosing.

Chapter summary

- The meaning of life is not something you find out there, but rather something you create inside of yourself.
- What's most meaningful to you is reflected in your values. Honoring your values will create happiness and life fulfillment, while chasing ever increasing goals and accomplishments will ultimately leave you dissatisfied.
- Values are "excavated" from within you and then clarified. They are not created overnight.
- The purpose of your life is what you decide it to be. Writing it down is a critical step.
- The foundation of a happy life and healthy

career is understanding and honoring your values, and living life "on purpose."

Coach's assignment

- Do the exercise of excavating your values.
- Go through the exercise of developing and writing down your life purpose statement.
- Reflect on the following questions: *Where in your life are you honoring your values? Where are you trampling on them? In what ways are you working and living life on purpose? In what ways are you compromising on that purpose?*

3

TAKE OFF THE MASK

Authenticity is a collection of choices that we have to make every day. It's about the choice to show up and be real. The choice to be honest. The choice to let our true selves be seen.

— BRENÉ BROWN

On a Sunday afternoon in high school, I was throwing a football with a friend in his front yard. It was a gorgeous Fall day in California, and in hindsight, I had absolutely nothing to worry about. Only I was worried. About what exactly I couldn't say, but it manifested as a general dread about going back to school the next morning. I was a good student, with lots of friends, and I enjoyed school. So why the worry? Part of it was simply not wanting to be cooped up and told what to do, but it was also more than that. I realize now that even as a well-adjusted, mostly happy kid, I sometimes had anxiety. In this case, it was anxiety about meeting all the expectations that came with school. Throwing the football with my friend, I was free. Sitting in class with authority figures running the show, I was constrained. Judging by the number of times I got sent to the Principal's office in school, I know I often acted out against that authority, but over time, the expectation to *fit in* sunk its claws into me.

The Sunday blues

Although that's not a very remarkable story, it's the earliest memory I have of what I call "the Sunday blues," that general feeling of not wanting to go back to work on Monday. It's got a complementary feeling in the TGIF sentiment, where you can't wait to get out of work on Friday to go home to your "personal life." As just about anyone could tell you, I was not unique in having those feelings.

But why is it like that? I recognize that it's not a universal feeling, as plenty of people can't wait to get back to work on Monday, but still it's surprisingly common. Setting aside the surface explanation that given the choice, we'd rather be sitting on a beach than working for the company, I think it's driven by something deeper.

Corporate employment, just like traditional school environments, is built on the expectation that people behave in certain ways. We learn pretty early that there are consequences for behaving outside of those expectations. Disrupt math class, get detention. Resist people you don't agree with, get labelled "difficult." Obviously, it works in the other direction too. Impress upper management, get a promotion. Display a can-do attitude, get labelled a "good team player." This puts pressure on us to show up in the way other people expect.

Putting on the mask

In order to be "successful" by society's standards, we learn to behave in ways expected of us, and for the most part, that's a good thing. It's what enables human beings to coordinate and collaborate on large-scale efforts. Without that ability, humankind might not have evolved beyond being tribes of hunters and gatherers. But the modern corporate world intensifies this expectation to conform—with its hiring processes, which look for "cultural fit," its performance review processes, which set "meets expectations" as the minimum measure of success, and its management hierarchy, which puts you under constant observation.

The consequences of not meeting expectations in the corporate world feel ominous. Getting to where you are now has not been easy. You have a lot invested in terms of education, years of experience, and reputation. You don't want to ruin it all by slipping up and getting yourself fired.

You don't want to feel the sting of failure, or the humiliation of public criticism, or the shame of not measuring up. This creates an ongoing need to be seen as someone who measures up, who won't get criticized, and who won't fail. So your guard goes up. You put on a metaphorical mask designed to give people the "correct" impression.

We wear the mask to fit in, to look the part that's expected of us. In the corporate world, we're expected to be smart and competent. We're expected to have a good attitude. We're expected not to get emotional, or dramatic. Well guess what? Humans don't know everything, they get in bad moods, they get emotional, and they create a lot of drama. We wear the mask to bridge the gap between what's happening on the inside and what we let the world see on the outside. *Never let 'em see you sweat. Fake it til you make it. Manage perception.* It's actually a big part of some leadership development programs to learn how to manage other people's perceptions of yourself.

Hiding what's on the inside

Of course, it's important to meet the expectations of your company. After all, they pay you, and you're entering into agreements about the type of work you'll do, what standards you'll meet, etc. I'm not suggesting you ignore those expectations. Those expectations are not the ones I'm talking about. On the inside, however, you are carrying around expectations about how you're supposed to show up.

See whether any of these thoughts sound familiar to you:

- *I don't want people to see how overwhelmed I'm feeling by the volume of work I'm juggling. I need to appear in control.*
- *I don't want people to see that I'm not busy. It will look like I'm not working hard enough, or that the company doesn't trust me with enough important work. I need to appear indispensable.*
- *I don't want to admit that I'm stumped about what to do next. I can't say "I don't know." I need to appear competent and in charge.*
- *This meeting is a complete waste of my time, but I need to suck it up and wait for it to end. I don't want to appear negative.*
- *This strategy is just another lame attempt that won't have any impact, but I won't say that out loud. I need to appear aligned and committed.*
- *I'm not nearly as talented (smart, strong, charismatic, insert your adjective) as the others in this room. They can see right through me. I need to appear more confident.*

I confess, I have felt each one of those sentiments at some point in my career. What each one has in common is an inner feeling that I wasn't comfortable letting others see. Implied in each of these statements is a belief about what's expected of me *as a person*. In addition to the tangible expectations about performing my job and executing on my deliverables, I'm trying to meet someone's expectations about *who I am* and *what I'm capable of*. I say "someone" because it's not crystal clear at first where those expectations come from. It's true, there are probably people in the organization who hold those expectations, but the feeling itself originates within me. I've internalized those expectations, and it didn't start when I got to the corporate world.

We start hearing the world's expectations of us as soon as we're old enough to understand them, from parents, teachers, and just about everyone else offering unsolicited advice. Over time, we internalize those expectations, carrying them around like a nagging voice in our head. When we inevitably fall short of perfection, it feels like a failure, but we keep up the appearance that everything is just fine. We don't want anyone to think we're not smart enough, or strong enough, fast enough, brave enough, charismatic enough, successful enough, good-looking enough, and on and on. To put it more succinctly, we don't want anyone to see us as "not enough." So we wear the mask to show we are enough.

In case you haven't noticed, this can be exhausting. It requires mental and emotional energy to maintain an outward impression that's different than your inward reality. It creates stress and anxiety. You go home tired at night, even though physically all you did was sit in an office environment all day. You can continue putting on this mask for the rest of your life if you're not careful. Or eventually, hopefully, you'll question whether you really need it. When that time comes, you can take off the mask.

Be vulnerable, be seen

The word "vulnerable" implies weakness for many people, and in some contexts, that's accurate. Achilles had a vulnerability in his heel. The Death Star had a vulnerability that allowed Luke Skywalker to blow it up. I'm not using the word in that way. There are many ways in which you should protect yourself. Wear a helmet while snowboarding. Don't touch the hot stove. Practice safe sex. Use caution and follow all safety procedures in your work.

I'm not going to suggest you make yourself vulnerable in situations where you should truly be protecting yourself, and you should never subject yourself to ongoing abuse, whether physical, mental, or emotional. However, beyond abuse and real danger, there are a whole lot of situations with the potential to cause us discomfort and even pain, where "protecting" ourselves may not be the best approach. For example, it stings when you get criticized. It's embarrassing when you make a mistake. It hurts when you get rejected. How many times have you thought of a question you wanted to ask in a meeting, but held your tongue because you felt like you should already know the answer? We instinctively protect ourselves from those types of discomfort, but it comes with a cost. It's difficult to get better at anything if you can't weather criticism. It's nearly impossible to accomplish anything meaningful if you're too afraid of making mistakes. And the cost of protecting yourself against rejection is hard to overestimate. Nothing worth achieving comes without the risk of failure or rejection.

It's not just the big things where this applies. To get where you are, you've taken this risk many times, whether throwing your hat in the ring for that big promotion or professing your love to another person. For those big life steps, we work up the courage and we take the step forward. Where it's more difficult to take this risk of being vulnerable is in our everyday way of being.

A couple years ago, I had a conversation with two coach colleagues. It was a slow time for my business and when asked how things were going, I openly shared that my business was not where I wanted it to be. I was wrestling with how to turn it around. In the past, this was just the sort of question I might have glossed over with "Oh, it's going great. All is good." Instead, I simply told the truth, not in a whiny way, or a victim kind of way, but in a matter-of-fact way. Their reactions were gratifying for me. The first one said she really appreciated hearing that from me, and then shared some of her own challenges.

The other agreed and said it was "disarming" to hear my honest answer. The word "disarming" struck me.

Why "disarming?" Because in truth, we usually have our guard up, ready to protect our ego. By not approaching it that way, I had a tangible impact on my two colleagues. I opened up an honest and useful dialogue, rather than just a surface conversation, which invited them to do the same. I let myself be seen. When the moment presented itself, I did not hide. Notice, I wasn't going out of my way to tell people how difficult things are, how my business is down, and woe is me, blah blah blah. I was simply honest—*in the moment that mattered*—and let myself be seen.

In my work with clients, I see how difficult it is, even for strong and talented executives, to allow themselves to be seen in emotionally honest ways. It takes courage. Many of them feel like it's a sign of weakness to experience emotions that convey anything other than confidence and authority. That leads to the mistaken belief that to be vulnerable is to be weak. Nothing could be further from the truth. The ability to be vulnerable is a sign of strength. Hiding your feelings so you avoid the discomfort of having them seen is a lot easier than being emotionally honest and accepting whatever discomfort comes along with it. I'm not suggesting you go around crying to others about your feelings. *I'm saying stop pretending you don't have feelings.*

You are enough

What would it mean to stop believing that you're not smart enough, or strong enough, or fast enough, or witty enough, or confident enough, or powerful enough? What would it mean to believe that you are already perfect, just the way you are? What would it mean to believe you are enough? I'll tell you what it would mean. It would mean you could stop trying to convince others that you are enough. Heck, it would mean you could stop trying to convince yourself that you are enough.

Is there something wrong with a cherry blossom bud on the tree that has not yet bloomed? Of course not. It's perfect the way it is, in that moment. It's right where it's supposed to be in its growth cycle. You are no different. You are a human being, and you are growing. The nature of human beings is that—in our emotional and mental growth cycle—we are messy. We experience emotion. We have irrational thoughts. We occasionally do stupid things. These are not signs there is something wrong with us. They're signs that we are human. Our evolution has left us hard-wired to experience a whole range of emotions, thoughts, and behaviors. It's just a byproduct of our human mind that we pretend otherwise.

This might seem like a paradox. If I'm already enough the way I am, why focus on self-improvement? This book and everything I'm about in my professional life is focused on growing as a person. The idea that you are already enough is not an excuse to be complacent and stop growing. It's a stand for the idea that no matter what inner struggles you're experiencing, no matter how far short of perfection you fall, you are not diminished as a human being. Nothing about you needs fixing. You can continue growing as a person for the rest of your life, not because there's some state of perfection you need to reach, but because that's the foundation of a fulfilling life. It's this journey of personal growth that gives life meaning. It's uniquely human and it's also the starting point for authentic leadership.

Lead with authenticity

I describe leading with authenticity on two levels. On one level, it means to *start* with authenticity, as in "lead off with authenticity." Your starting place in any leadership endeavor should be one of transparency and honesty. Let's say you get a big promotion, and as soon as the announcement goes out, you start feeling some anxiety about how challenging this role will be and how much you have to learn. When you start interacting with your key stakeholders (boss, employees, peers, etc.), how do you show up? Most of us understand intuitively that we should be confident, so that's how we try to show up. But we do that by pretending not to have any anxiety. To lead with authenticity would mean being honest with our stakeholders that we don't know everything and have a lot to learn. Besides being an excellent demonstration of humility—a critical practice in authentic leadership—it's also honest. More importantly, it's a sign of being confident, the very thing we wanted to project in the first place. Pretending to have it all under control when that's not really what we feel on the inside is a sure sign of insecurity. It's also a sign of insecurity to go on and on to anyone who will listen that you're anxious and don't have all the answers. That's seeking external validation (i.e., looking for others to reassure you that you're good enough). What I'm preaching here is simply to be seen honestly. That's the strength of vulnerability that I described earlier.

On this level, another way that leading with authenticity might appear is when a conflict arises between you and another person, which creates some tension. My weakness in this regard is email. There was a time when I couldn't resist sending back an aggressive zinger whenever I got an email that pissed me off. It always felt good to do it, but almost immediately afterward, I would feel regret. So to counter that, I would work on not reacting, but all that did was drive my anger (or resentment, or whatever the feeling was) back inside of me—where it festered as a general negative feeling toward the other person.

I had the opportunity to lead with authenticity in an email exchange just this week with a colleague. We serve together on a board of directors and are collaborating on a project to upgrade our board's document management systems. We have very different styles, as I tend to move forward aggressively and she is more cautious. That tension led to an email exchange over the weekend where she wanted me to slow down with what I was doing. I didn't receive the message very well and got overly annoyed and defensive. I could have stewed about it, reinforcing negative feelings toward my colleague, or worse, I could have fired off an email defending my position and pointing out how misinformed I think she is. Instead, I waited a few hours and responded with a short, honest description of my feelings. There was no blaming, no defensiveness, just owning up to the impact that her email had on me and owning the feelings. That didn't "solve" the problem—it just opened up space for real dialogue to occur between us. The next morning, we had a conversation that was so powerful it transformed our working relationship. I could have avoided the issue or lashed out against her, either of which would have corroded the relationship. Instead, we made a dramatic step forward in the way we balance our different styles. By making my first action in the conflict to let my genuine feelings be seen, I was leading with authenticity.

On a more general level, leading with authenticity means being open and letting yourself be seen on a regular basis. Corporate life is chock full of situations where leaders think they need to hide their feelings. I teach a coaching model to corporate leaders that includes a tool for structuring their coaching conversations. The tool is on a laminated card and includes some additional handouts for note taking, etc. In every class, when I challenge them to practice this model when they return to their teams, they bring up their discomfort at trying something new with their team. They worry about having the card and other materials visible while they practice this new skill and think they should keep what they're doing private. My answer is always "*No!* Let people see the tool you're using. Tell them you're practicing a new skill. If it feels a little awkward, share this with them." You don't need to fool people about what you're doing and feeling. Be transparent with what you're doing and why. Say "I'm practicing some new coaching skills; do you mind if I use this tool while we have our conversation? What's that, you're wondering what it is? Well, let me show you…" That's what confident people do.

Another area I spend a lot of time on with clients is their need to be the one with all the answers. If you carry this expectation around, then you live in constant fear that someone will ask you a question you can't answer. Certainly, you should be prepared in your job, do your research, and do everything you can to stay current and competent in the work you do. But the smarter and more experienced you get, the more you understand how much *you don't know*. Being able to admit it when you don't know takes confidence. Most importantly, if you want the people around you to open up, to collaborate, and to share what they know (or don't know), it's best not to suck up all the oxygen trying to prove how much you know.

As part of a larger leadership development program, I do some group coaching with front line supervisors at a large transportation company. I am somewhat of an authority figure to them because I'm positioned as the expert on the training they're getting from the organization. My job is to help them assimilate the material and put it into practice. Of course, they push back on some of the content and resist trying new approaches. The way I show up with them is not to force these ideas on them, but to listen to their perspectives and be open and honest about what I think and feel about the content they are learning. I find that it opens people up to think differently and try new things. I'm never critical of the content, but I am transparent about my own struggles or challenges to make sense of certain ideas. The most gratifying feedback I get from these participants, both verbally and in writing, is that they see me as "real." One guy told me at the end of the program, "You're like a real person." It made me laugh, but it also touched me deeply. Being authentically me has a positive impact that being a corporate guy just can't match.

To be "authentic" is to be fully expressed as who you are, not who you wish you were, or who you think others expect you to be. Taking off the mask of invulnerability is being real. Leading with authenticity is the foundation of your liberation.

Chapter summary

- The world puts expectations on us and we feel pressure to conform.
- Rather than let the world see our uniqueness, we put on a metaphorical mask designed to make us fit in. We're afraid that not doing this would risking criticism, failure, and shame.
- We internalize those expectations into beliefs about how we're supposed to be, and we carry those beliefs around unwittingly.
- The mask is like a protective guard, and its opposite is vulnerability. Vulnerability is not a weakness; it's a sign of strength and confidence. It requires courage to let yourself be seen in emotionally honest ways.
- Believing you are enough is what enables you to be vulnerable.
- Being vulnerable and believing you are enough is at the heart of authentic leadership. Leading with authenticity means being open and honest with yourself and others about what you feel.

Coach's assignment

- Reflect on this question: What are my deepest

feelings that I would prefer never to share?
What is the fear that keeps this hidden?

- Catch yourself wearing the mask. For one
  week, once a day, write down a situation where
  you didn't let your true feelings be seen. Before
  the week is over, challenge yourself to let
  yourself be seen in an authentic way at
  least once.

PART II

CONNECT

You've shown up, as a leader, with courage, purpose, and authenticity. This alone has raised your impact, but it's time to deepen your impact. You have immense power at your fingertips, though you may not understand that yet. Like any power source, you need to connect to it. It's either on or off; you are either connected or disconnected. It's important to understand that connection is a state of being. You won't always be connected, but you can learn to understand what being connected means, notice when you've disconnected, and reconnect at will.

4

LEAD PEOPLE, MANAGE THINGS

Management is doing things right; leadership is doing the right things.

— PETER DRUCKER

In one of my earliest jobs after I finished graduate school, I had an experience that has stuck with me ever since. It wasn't a particularly profound experience, but it caused me some anxiety at the time and it taught me about a theme I see popping up again and again with executives.

I was part of a very small company—my boss was the owner—and we were attending a Myers Briggs Type Indicator (MBTI) workshop together. We were a contractor to a large government agency who was sponsoring the workshop. If you're familiar with Myers Briggs, you know it's a personality assessment that measures things like how we process information, and how we make decisions. I've taken the MBTI four or five times in my career since then, but that was my first. During the course of the day, we participated in various exercises designed to give us insight into our type. In one particular problem-solving exercise, I was paired with my boss, and as luck would have it, I saw the solution to our problem very quickly. Being an eager 20-something ready to impress his boss, I dove in immediately with the solution. Imagine my surprise when I discovered she couldn't see that solution and didn't agree that it was the right way forward. At first, I was dumbfounded. *How could she not see it?!* Obviously, I just needed to explain it better, stick to my guns, and she would see. But the more I tried, the more she resisted, until my frustration showed and the seeds of my learning were planted.

We had a good facilitator who was able to use our example to illustrate how differences in personality type can result in conflicts such as these. At the time, I wasn't mature enough to fully absorb that lesson. I was still frustrated because we had failed at the task. I could see that we had success in our sights—until my boss got in the way. *I was right damn it! Don't give me this touchy-feely bullshit about getting along together and adjusting our personality styles for each other. She's the problem!* That's how I felt at the time anyway.

It took much longer for the real learning to sink in from the experience. Obviously, it didn't matter that I had the right solution if my boss was not on board. Simply having the right answer was not enough. In the 24 years since that day, I would experience that lesson again and again in various ways. And I've learned from countless executive clients that I am not alone in experiencing it.

Before I explain this a little deeper, let me separate out an additional but related learning point: I am not always right. Yes, I admit it, and my wife will tell you I still haven't learned it, but I know it's true. Being able to see when we're wrong, slowing down enough to listen and see that we could be wrong—that's an incredibly important thing to learn. In this chapter, I'm dealing with a different point. Whether we're right or wrong is less important than what impact we are having on the person we want to influence. In solving a math problem, there is only one right answer. In solving a human problem, such as a disagreement, a conflicting perspective, or even a different understanding of the answer to the math problem, much more is required.

Managing "things" is relatively easy. Managing people is hard as hell. People are messy. People don't always respond consistently or even logically. So quit trying to interact with them as if they were things.

People are not the problem

Compare these two responses to a common scenario. An employee who works for you has been showing up late to work, seems disengaged in meetings, and is not performing anywhere near what you need. One response begins with the thought: *Bob is slacking off, being lazy, and generally bringing the team down. If I don't nip this in the bud, I'm going to have problems. What makes him think I don't notice, and why does he think he can get away with it?* You decide to address the issue directly, and you start the conversation by telling him what he's doing wrong and why that's a problem for you. You are ready to prove your point with examples and evidence.

Another response begins with this thought: *I get the sense that Bob's having some difficulty meeting his job requirements right now. Whatever is causing it, it probably doesn't feel great for him. He might not realize that I'm noticing, and he might be stuck in some way.* You decide to address the issue directly, and you start the conversation by telling him what you've noticed and how you're concerned about him and his success in the role. You're ready to listen and understand his experience of the situation.

What's the difference? In both examples, the structure of the conversation is similar, but your *way of being*, both before and during the conversation is different. Consider each scenario. How open are you likely to be in understanding his experience? What kind of energy do you think you'll be projecting? How do you think Bob is likely to respond in each scenario? In neither case are you ignoring the problem, but maybe you're seeing the problem in a different way. In the first scenario, the problem is Bob. In the second scenario, the problem is

Bob's behavior. It's the difference between trying to fix Bob and trying to fix the situation. This may sound counterintuitive, but the person is never the problem. How they are behaving, what they are saying, and what circumstances they are creating—those are all legitimate problems to be addressed.

The natural outcome of treating the person as the problem is that you need to control the person. Unfortunately, short of using coercion and manipulation, you cannot control others. Maybe it's no surprise then that corporate life is full of coercion and manipulation. Don't believe me? At its essence, what is the dynamic behind the words: "You have to do what I say because I'm your boss, we pay you, and we can fire you at will"? Usually that sentiment is put much more tactfully, but nevertheless it's what's lurking under the surface in hierarchical organizations. To my ear, no matter how much you sugarcoat it, there's no way to argue that's anything other than coercion. The very phrase "people management," which is commonplace in corporate life, implies control.

When you become a people manager, you are in charge of deciding many things about people's lives, including their salary, bonus percentages, work assignments, etc. I've heard many managers say they don't like this part of their job. It can be the source of much frustration because people usually follow one of two paths: either they try to please everyone and fail miserably, or they become a hard-ass control-freak and eventually fail miserably. To avoid the failure, those managers try harder, increasingly falling back on manipulation and coercion. The manager who can't please everyone attempts to spin everything as positively as possible, trying to manipulate people's feelings. The manager who resorts to hierarchical authority to enforce their will is practicing coercion. In the short run, this can achieve compliance, but in the long run, neither of these approaches is effective.

This is a difficult lesson for many leaders, and it seems antithetical to what we're often taught leadership is about. *Isn't getting people to do what I need done what leadership is all about?* No, actually, it's not. That's management. Managing is excellent for controlling processes, like inventory tracking, or product testing, but it has inherent limits when applied to living, breathing, feeling people.

The people who are good at getting people to follow are the ones who end up in "leadership positions" most frequently. After all, they're doing something right to have that kind of influence in the first place. The problem arises when they run up against resistance, which they always will if they are seeking to create something that represents a change to the status quo. So they push harder, trying to control.

Think of a sales manager who wants their sales reps to adopt a new sales life cycle process they successfully used at a previous company. Excited to create some positive results, they enthusiastically roll out the process at the monthly sales team meeting. There are some initial objections about how our business doesn't really fit with that process, how the reps don't have the resources and support to follow that process, etc., but the manager pushes on anyway, thinking *I know if they just do, it they'll see the value.*

A month later, the manager is disappointed at how little has changed in the way the reps are managing their accounts. The manager doubles down, makes the process mandatory, and implements a reporting mechanism for the reps to document their activities. Pretty soon, resentment starts to bubble up among the sales reps. Some simply don't do the documentation, others start spending all their time documenting what a great job they're doing, and the manager scratches their head, wondering why this team can't figure out how to make good use of this great process.

Another approach is to let go of the need to change your colleague's behavior and shift your attention to your colleague as a person. *What are they focused on? What are their goals? What do they need, what do they want, what are they afraid of?* The corporate world has conditioned us to focus on getting results, which is understandable, but standing between me and the results I want are people. You don't have to answer those questions by yourself—*you can ask!* Rather than telling them to change their behavior, start by asking them about themselves. Be genuinely curious about them and why they behave the way they do.

As much as we wish it were not so, we cannot change other people's behavior. Even if you force people to change, they've only changed because they fear the consequences. So if you want different behavior from someone, you have to impact the person in a different way. It's counter-intuitive to most, but the answer is *stop trying to control people*. When you let go of trying to control people, you feel like you've lost something (um, like control?). It feels like you've given up your power. I believe it's the opposite. By acknowledging you don't control people, and letting go of your power *over* people, you open a conduit to a deeper source of power, which is what we'll look at next.

Connect to your power center

The power vested in you by external sources, like moving up the org chart, is inherently limited. It feels like it's all the power you need, because in effect, it gives you the power to control people. If I had a nickel for every corporate executive who said to me "I could be more successful if only that team of people over there were reporting to me," well, I'd have a lot more nickels in my pocket. When it does happen, they're often surprised that their problems are not solved as easily as they hoped. They mistakenly believe that if they can control those "resources" (i.e., people), their challenges will be solved. Ask any chief executive how true that is in reality.

The power I want to talk to you about is not something given to you by an org chart, a job, or a piece of paper. I'm talking about the power center that resides inside of you, if only you tap into it.

The previous chapters of this book illustrated how you can charge up this power source.

- Courageously choose to be a leader
- Define and follow your sense of purpose
- Take off the mask and be authentic

All those steps charge you up and empower you, which by itself can transform your life. However, I assume you picked up this book because you want to make a difference in your workplace. To do that, you must use your power to create **impact** on people.

What kind of impact can you have on people? Well, you can have an impact on people's behavior, but that's the most difficult impact to have directly, which is why we end up resorting to coercion and manipulation. There are too many intervening variables affecting people's behavior. You can impact what people *think*, which is a little easier, but still a challenge because we don't all think alike and we don't easily change our beliefs. This is why we enjoy managing the people who think like we do, but we get frustrated by those who don't.

Or you can impact the way people *feel*. Impacting how people feel is relatively easy. In fact, most of the time you do it without even thinking about it. My wife asks me how her new shoes look, and I absentmindedly mumble that they look fine. Do you think I've impacted how she feels? See, I'm a master at this. That example, however, is an example of how I am wasting my power. If what I want is a loving, healthy marriage, then making her feel angry, resentful, or ignored works against me. If on the other hand, I'm present enough to hear her ask and take the time to look and give her my heartfelt truthful answer, I'm injecting positive power into the situation. I'm empowering our marriage.

Corporate life is not a marriage, but it is based on relationships, and marriage is simply a prime example. Corporate life—i.e., organizational life—is built on relationships. I don't mean that relationships are an important part of organizational life. I mean that organizational life is comprised *entirely* of relationships. If you want to have impact in your organization, you better get more intentional about the impact you're having in your working relationships.

What I find in organizations is that many leaders are not aware of, or worse—don't care about the impact they have on people's feelings. They would rationalize this sentiment by saying something like "I don't have time to worry about people's feelings" or "He needs to suck it up; we're not running a kindergarten here." What these statements represent is an obliviousness to the impact one is having. You can say all you want that feelings don't have any place in business, but all you're doing is lying to yourself. The only way feelings are not present in the workplace is if all the humans have been replaced by robots. Wouldn't you rather be intentional about tapping into this power source than simply wasting it, or letting it work against you?

That's the part you *can* change. You can become much more aware of the impact you are having on people, how you're making them feel, and if you're aware of it, you can begin to harness it and direct it. This is the root of your personal power.

Earlier, we covered choosing love over fear. Both love and fear have power. Adolph Hitler was an enormously effective leader, in terms of the impact he created, using his ability to make people feel a certain way, but it was rooted in fear. Jesus Christ is arguably the greatest leader of all time, certainly by the standard of impact he had on the world, and his was a message of love. Over the following 2,000 years, many people have perverted that message into one based in fear, but that's a topic for another book. The point is this: you have tremendous power by virtue of how you make other people feel. You can be intentional about using your personal power in service of all that is good, or in service of all that is evil, or you can waste your power by not even paying attention. If you want to liberate your inner leader and be happy at work, make an impact by showing the love.

There are many ways to impact how other people feel. Those ways will almost always be conveyed via your words, your actions, and your choices. The place I want to encourage you to start practicing this power is in the art of conversation.

Engage the power of conversation

What I do for a living, essentially, is to have conversations. People are often surprised when I tell them my coaching will not really be about training them to do something or telling them what to do. If I'm not going to be the expert and give them the knowledge and expertise they need, then what are they paying me for? The answer is: focused and powerful conversations. While I do bring my leadership expertise into the dialogue, it is of secondary importance, especially since near-infinite information is readily available at your fingertips within seconds.

It's conversation that carries the power. Conversation is the strongest tool in your leadership toolbox, in your *life* toolbox for that matter. So why aren't you using it more? One answer is that when your focus is on controlling others, conversation just serves to remind you that you have no real control over others. Another reason is that conversation quickly gets uncomfortable for a lot of people, because it elicits emotion, vulnerability, and intimacy. When done well, it can get very real, very quickly, and as I've just described, that's where you have real power.

I'm not talking about ordinary, casual conversation. Most everyday conversation is surface level and leaves enormous amounts of information unsaid. We mask how we feel and hide what we truly think, for a variety of reasons, many of which have been mentioned in the previous chapters. That's why when we connect with someone in meaningful dialogue, where the stakes matter, it feels different. Speaking with each other about our project plan is different than speaking with each other about how we just sniped at each other in that project meeting. We either avoid the latter, or we turn it into an aggressive confrontation, neither of which is constructive. The power of real dialogue, on the other hand, lies in stripping away the facade and defensiveness and getting real. It's about making what's hidden in the conversation visible, including assumptions. Real dialogue seeks to get all the information out on the table, including the emotional information.

One of the best books out there on this topic is *Crucial Conversations*, by Kerry Patterson, et al. In it, the authors describe this process as creating a shared pool of meaning between participants. We're always creating meaning out of circumstances, words, and actions, in the form of assumptions, thoughts, and beliefs. Imagine if we could be explicit about the meaning we're creating while we have the conversation. Well, we can be. It might be awkward at first, and it can be downright scary, but it's a powerful thing to do.

In coaching sessions where my client is dealing with a challenging situation involving another person, one of the outcomes we arrive at is almost always for my client to go and have an important conversation with that person.

This power of conversation goes both ways. Not only can you have an impact on how other people feel, but you can transform the way you yourself feel. I once had a client who kept clashing with his boss over the right approach to whatever he was working on and he was on the verge of quitting. He kept telling me his boss didn't trust him and didn't think he was very good at his job. I asked him how he knew that and I heard story after story about how the boss micromanaged him, made decisions that went against his wishes, and generally was "out to get him." Again, I kept pressing, how did he know that? While he could point to all kinds of evidence to validate his belief, he couldn't actually say that he knew for certain what was driving his boss. So he committed to starting a dialogue with his boss about how this behavior was impacting him.

The effect was immediate. My client went into the conversation owning his own feelings, not accusing the boss of anything, and opened up about what he was experiencing and how it felt. The boss was surprised to hear it, because he thought very highly of my client. When my client explained which behaviors made him feel this way, the boss opened up about how he'd wrestled with this for much of his career. It wasn't the first time he'd gotten the feedback. Like a lot of executives, this boss had high standards and a lot of knowledge about how to meet those standards. He genuinely thought he was helping my client by giving him so much direction. When my client opened the dialogue the way he did, honestly and without criticizing, it enabled his boss to be open about his own feelings, without getting defensive.

In this particular case, the boss did not change his behavior overnight, but the impact on my client was enormous. He told me it was like a giant weight being lifted off him, because he no longer had to spend energy worrying about why his boss was "out to get him." That is the more important point. You can't control other people's behavior, but you can transform *how you feel* in response to other people's behavior, and that gives you the power to better affect how other people feel. Over time, the relationship between my client and his boss steadily improved, because they now had the ability to address their issues directly, with emotional honesty, through the power of conversation.

Having these conversations is not easy, because if we're not practiced in it, it can feel awkward and downright scary. It requires courage to choose such a conversation, which is what we covered in *Chapter 1, Be a Leader*. It requires a sense of purpose to pursue a bigger vision for our relationship than what we are currently experiencing (*Chapter 2, Decide Why You're Here*). And most importantly, it requires the ability to open up, authentically, about what we're experiencing and feeling, like we covered in *Chapter 3, Take Off the Mask*.

You can transform your world with conversation. It's the vehicle for your personal power, and it's at the heart of leading people. You can't have a conversation with things, and you shouldn't "manage people," but you can lead people and manage things.

Chapter summary

- Human beings are complex. They do not always behave predictably or logically.
- People are not problems. Their behavior, on the other hand, can be very problematic.
- Treating people as the problem leads to the need to control people, which boils down to manipulation and coercion.
- Let go of the need to control people and lean into the practice of understanding people.
- The biggest power you have with people is your ability to impact the way they feel. The influence you wield in your organization is centered largely on this ability.
- The tool to wield this power is conversation. Engaging in powerful conversations is at the heart of leading people.

Coach's assignment

- Interrupt one of your email threads and pick up the phone for a real conversation.
- Go and start one of the conversations you know you need to have, but have been avoiding. Take off the mask and open up with what you're feeling.

5

BE PRESENT

What is real? How do you define 'real'? If you're talking about what you can feel, what you can smell, what you can taste and see, then 'real' is simply electrical signals interpreted by your brain.

— MORPHEUS

One of my all-time favorite movies is *The Matrix*. If you're not familiar with it, or just don't remember it, I'll refresh your memory. The hero of the story is Neo, a computer hacker who has always had this nagging sense that something isn't quite right with reality. He finds himself targeted by the police, as well as some black-suited, earpiece-wearing, sunglass-clad agents trying to kill him. Before he can be captured, he's rescued by Morpheus, who offers him a choice. Morpheus explains that none of what Neo is experiencing is real. Reality is just an illusion. Morpheus offers Neo two pills. Take the red pill and all will be revealed. Take the blue pill and everything will return to normal, life will go on, and he will be oblivious to the truth. Neo chooses the red pill, which sets in motion a bizarre set of events where we learn that Neo's physical body is not where he thought it was. Rather, it's sitting in a cocoon-like pod, along with millions of other human bodies. This vast network of human bodies is maintained by a malevolent artificial intelligence that has taken over the world. The world he awakens into is nothing like the world he's been experiencing his whole life. The life he's known since birth was an illusion, lived purely in his head.

This is not an original story. Around 2,400 years ago, the Greek philosopher Plato wrote the allegory of the cave in *The Republic*. In Plato's story, we imagine a group of humans living in a cave. They are chained in such a way that they cannot turn to face the opening of the cave, and can only face the back wall. While they cannot see the world outside the cave, they are able to see the shadows of the world, cast upon the wall of their cave. Every experience they have of the world is perceived through shadows. Plato argues that if the prisoners were suddenly freed, they would likely stumble into the bright outside world and be terrified, only to return as quickly as possible to the safety of the cave, much like one of the characters in *The Matrix*, who exclaims at one point: "I should have taken the blue pill!"

What does any of this have to do with liberating your inner leader to escape Corporate Hell, you wonder? *What if I told you that Corporate Hell is just an illusion?*

We're about to get deep, so you may want to grab a cup of coffee and open your mind as wide as you can. I'm here to offer you the red pill.

It's all in your head

What Plato was getting at is that we rarely experience the world directly. Our minds are spectacularly efficient meaning-making machines. We constantly perceive a massive amount of stimuli, more than we could ever possibly pay attention to. Millions of bits of data enter our senses every second, and near-instantly, our mind makes sense of it, filtering out most of it, and translating the data into labels, concepts, judgments, and conclusions. Think about that for a minute. How do you *experience* that translation of data into meaning? It's in the form of *thoughts*, of course. You think. All the time.

You are so immersed in thinking that you don't even realize you're doing it. You experience it as perceiving events directly, which leads to a strange idea. You become *identified with* your own thoughts. You fall for the illusion that you are your thoughts, that what you are thinking is what is actually happening all around you. But it's not true.

There's someone in your head, but it's not you

Reflect on this question of how you experience your thoughts and you'll soon realize you have a voice in your head. More accurately, you probably have multiple voices in your head, each for a different mood or set of circumstances. In my professional and personal experience, I have yet to meet someone who doesn't have such a voice in their head. If you're thinking to yourself right now, "I don't know what he's talking about, I don't have a voice in my head," well guess what? That's the voice talking.

When I say you "identify" with the thoughts in your head, what I mean is you take the voice in your head to be you. You "think" that the voice in your head is you. You think that everything happening to the voice is happening to you. The problem with that perspective is that it's wrong.

The voice in your head is nothing more than a construct of your mind. Yes, it's the thing that evolved in humans that enabled us to conquer the world, but nevertheless, it's a fiction in your head. Our ability to think, to represent the world in abstract concepts generated solely by the firing of neurons in our brains, is uniquely human. And it's powerful.

What does your inner voice have to say? It tells you what's important and what's not. It tells you how great you are (*I'm so proud to be publishing my first book*), how stupid you are (*How could I have been so stupid!*), how lucky you are, how cursed you are, whether you're in danger, and on and on. When you look at it that way, you can see that you are experiencing the world indirectly, through the narrative of your thoughts.

Listen to the sentence structure I've been using. The *voice* is telling *you* something. The voice is the subject and you are the object. Are there two of you? Judging by the internal dialogue going on in my head on any given day, it seems there are, but that's insane. Yet all humans seem to suffer from this same insanity. This notion is called Dualism and it's been described in ancient spiritual traditions going back as far as we have recorded history.

It's been described in modern writings as well, including in the *Inner Game* books by former Harvard Psychology professor turned coach Timothy Gallwey. The "Inner Game" refers to this central idea that we experience the world through the inner voice of our thoughts. Gallwey called the dual selves Self 1 and Self 2. Self 1 is a chattering loudmouth, constantly running his mouth off, criticizing, proclaiming success and failure, telling you what to fear and who to fear, and generally being a pain in the butt. Self 2 is the one listening. Gallwey explains how it is Self 2 who performs, whether on the tennis court or at work, and to the degree that Self 2 can ignore Self 1— performance improves. Self 2 is the real self, the one who truly exists beyond the conceptual "I" of our thoughts.

Rick Carson called this fictional entity in our heads a "gremlin" in his entertaining and highly practical book

Taming Your Gremlin. In another profoundly insightful book —*The Untethered Soul* by Michael Singer—the voice is compared to an inner roommate, and I would add, an inner roommate from hell. Pay attention and you will begin to see how much power this voice has in your life.

The depth of this insight goes far beyond what I can cover in this book (but I highly recommend reading the books I've just mentioned if you're interested in learning more). The point I want you to take away now is that the voice in your head is not you, and the more you identify with that voice, the more disconnected you are from your true self, from who you truly are.

That sets up the profound question: if you're not who you *think* you are, then who exactly are you?

You are one with the Universe

Carl Sagan, in his 1980s-era TV show *Cosmos*, said "The nitrogen in our DNA, the calcium in our teeth, the iron in our blood, the carbon in our apple pies were made in the interiors of collapsing stars." That idea has long resonated with me, but it's a related thing he said that had a deep effect on me spiritually. He said "The cosmos is within us. We are made of star stuff. We are a way for the Universe to know itself." *I am a way for the Universe to know itself?* Of course I am. Humanity was not beamed here from another planet, nor placed here fully formed by a supreme being. Life, and by extension Homo Sapiens, evolved out of the elements on Earth, beginning almost 4 billion years ago. The Earth evolved with the cosmos, beginning almost 14 billion years ago after the Big Bang, and it's been unfolding ever since. All of it, the whole enchilada, is one big emerging reality, with elements continually taking new forms. When you see the Universe in this way, the truth of Carl Sagan's words hit home. ***I am the Universe, conscious of itself.*** My fleshy bag of bones is a pretty small part of the Universe, but the important point is that I am not *separate* from the Universe.

I promise this is about as deep as I'm going to get in this book, but it's relevant. We feel like we're alone in this world. We sit behind our eyes, living in the illusion that this voice in our head (what we think of as "I") is separate from everything and everyone else around us. We think no one else feels what we feel. We think others are better than us, or that we're better than others. We compare ourselves, we criticize ourselves, and we celebrate ourselves. We fight with others, give others the cold shoulder, or simply "otherize" others. In short, we live in isolation from each other. Too harsh? I don't think so. It's not always like this, because if it were, we'd have no way of knowing it was true. It's in those rare moments when we break the isolation and genuinely connect—with our true self, with the natural world around us, and with others—that we truly understand.

What I've learned is that most humans spend much of their lives in a state of disconnection and separation. The ongoing dialogue happening inside the mind is actually the source of most human suffering. I don't mean the very real pain and suffering that comes as a result of tragedy and physical, emotional, and mental abuse. What I do mean is that the incessant stream of thinking in our head is the source of what most humans suffer from on a daily basis. Around 2,500 years ago, the Buddha said "Life is Suffering." This phrase is often misunderstood, but what he meant was that suffering comes from this illusion of separation—the illusion of a separate thinking self. What I discovered about Corporate Hell is that so much of the dissatisfaction—i.e., the "suffering"—comes from this inner dialogue of the thinking self.

Become aware of your thinking self

How aware are you of your thinking self? It's one thing to read about it, but it's quite another to experience it. Let's try a quick experiment to get a glimpse of it. For the next full minute, I want you to close your eyes and pay atten-tion to your breathing. Notice the breath coming in through your nose, filling your lungs, and going out, exhaling through your mouth. Set a timer for one minute and keep your attention on your breathing. Do it now; I'll wait.

How did it go? If you noticed your mind wandering before the minute was up, consider it a success. The purpose of this exercise is not to try to make it the whole minute without thinking. The point is to feel the difference between being fully present, like when you were following your breathing, and when you're not, like when your mind wandered. Noticing how your attention can be here one moment and somewhere else the next was the point.

This exercise is a microcosm of how we spend most of our life. We are sometimes fully present, but mostly, we spend our lives in our head, thinking about the world, rather than experiencing it directly. We don't realize it because so much of the way we operate can be done automatically. When you learned to drive, you were very much in the present, but now, you can get in your car, drive across town, park, and get out, all without paying any conscious attention to the task. This can hold true for interpersonal tasks too. Have you ever sat in a meeting, appearing on the outside to have all the signs of paying close attention, yet when someone calls your name, you instantly return from a faraway place in your head, not having heard what was said at all?

The effect can be more subtle in a one-to-one interaction between you and another person. You're nodding in all the right places, saying things when you're expected to, and appearing on the outside to be present and listening. But on the inside, you're carrying on your own dialogue about what you think of the other person, what you're going to say next, why they're wrong (or right), etc. You're sitting right across from the other person, but you're really not present.

It's like you're watching a dramatized version of events, rather than experiencing the actual events directly. You're able to interact directly with the drama, but you've got a running commentary going on in the background, constantly stirring the pot of your thoughts and feelings. When you're in a meeting lost in your own thoughts, it's when someone says your name and asks you a question that the drama in your head suddenly stops and you're back in the present moment. What I want you to grasp is an understanding of that feeling.

What's important is that you recognize how pervasively you experience the world through the voice in your head, and that you also recognize how that spell can be broken. You can **become present**. Being present is not actually the hard part. Getting better at *recognizing when you are not present* and in that moment *becoming present*—that is the harder work to be done. It takes practice.

Practicing presence through mindfulness meditation

There is really only one way to practice this skill and that is to pay attention. By itself, I know that sounds a little vague. However, I mean something very specific. To intentionally, and even systematically, pay attention to the wandering nature of your mind, and repeatedly practice bringing your attention back to the present moment—that is the practice of mindfulness meditation.

My first real experience with mindfulness meditation came in my mid-twenties. I was working for a well-known medical center in New York City and was in charge of our community wellness program. We offered health and wellness programs to the public, and in my first year, I got to experience the Mindfulness-based Stress Reduction Program. The program was created by Jon Kabat-Zinn at the University of Massachusetts Medical Center as a treatment for chronic pain and stress. To understand the program, I participated in eight weeks of mindfulness meditation practice, capped off by a silent retreat, where the other participants and I spent a full day together with no talking or communication of any kind among us. The program was an experience that gave a big shove on the rudder of my life. It didn't transform me overnight into a meditation guru and I didn't pack up and move to Nepal to join a monastery. But I did discover the power of practicing mindfulness. I discovered that my mental state is fluid and that I have the power to influence my own state of mind.

Many people are turned off by the idea of meditation because they believe it's a mysterious religious practice. While it's true that many Eastern religions and spiritual traditions, such as Buddhism, have meditation at their core, there is absolutely no reason why the benefits of mindfulness meditation can't be harnessed in a completely secular way. That was the case with the program I participated in, and it's the case with the enormous movement today to bring mindfulness into the mainstream. Companies such as Google, General Mills, Target, and Aetna have learned the power of mindfulness and have created programs to support their employees in building a mindfulness meditation practice. U.S. Congressman Tim Ryan from Ohio has become a practitioner of mindfulness meditation and wrote a book *A Mindful Nation: How a Simple Practice Can Help Us Reduce Stress, Improve Performance, and Recapture the American Spirit.* In his book, Congressman Ryan makes a compelling case for bringing mindfulness into our schools, boardrooms, and governmental institutions in service of creating a better future.

You don't have to join anything or adopt any beliefs in order to practice mindfulness. You don't have to do any esoteric rituals or seek some trance-like state of consciousness. Mindfulness meditation is none of that. It's what I said earlier: the practice of paying attention to how your mind works and becoming present. You can do this for five minutes while mindfully eating a box of raisins, or by sitting in a chair for 30 minutes with your eyes closed, or by participating in a retreat for a week. It's not defined by the format, but rather by the activity itself of mindfully paying attention in the present moment.

I won't spend time going in-depth about how to do mindfulness meditation, because it's beyond the scope of this book, and more importantly, it's not something you can learn from reading. You have to experience it, which you did for one minute earlier in this chapter. If you want to learn mindfulness meditation, there are countless ways to do that, from a slew of mobile apps hitting the market to online programs to courses you might find in your city or town.

The important question to answer here is why would you want to practice mindfulness in the first place? There are two main answers to that question. First, getting a better handle on your own mind, including the "I-focused" voice in your head that has a life of its own, will lead you to have more equanimity in your life. That means you won't be knocked off your game so easily when things go wrong, and let's face it, life in the corporate world is full of situations that feel like they've gone wrong. You will, in a very real sense, be happier and more content when you're not so easily pushed around by the chattering voice in your head.

The second answer to the question of "why practice mindfulness," is that it makes you a far more powerful leader. Cultivating presence in yourself makes you a better, more patient listener and will raise the level of impact you have on others, because *having presence* is something that people around you can feel.

Having executive presence

In my corporate career, I've led countless "talent calibration sessions" where senior executives discuss the strengths and weaknesses of the people working for them. A term that always gets tossed around in those meetings is "executive presence." It seems easy to say who has it and who doesn't, but it's much more difficult for those executives to describe exactly *what it is* and *how one gets it.* In fact, most executives I know come to the conclusion that it's something people are born with, not something they can learn. While it's true that executive presence comes more naturally to some than others, it's not a fixed trait. Having presence is simply what results from being present consistently enough for people to notice it and feel it.

In today's highly distracted culture, having presence is a big advantage to you as a leader. Conventional wisdom tells you to put your phone down when speaking with others and to turn away from your computer when someone comes into your office. This is excellent advice; do everything you can to eliminate distractions when they get between you and other people. The bigger point of this chapter is that you also have a major distraction living inside your own head. Being present means quieting that voice and getting out of your own head.

In the remaining chapters, there are many ideas that rest on top of this foundation of presence. It can be challenging to do many of the things I'm going to share without having presence. For that reason, it's critical that you keep practicing. Gaining mastery over your own mind takes practice, but the rewards are big.

Chapter summary

- The nature of the human mind is such that most of our experience with the world comes through the prism of our own thoughts.
- The constant thread of our thoughts manifests as a voice in our heads. We mistake that voice to be who we are, our concept of self, so to speak.
- Who we are, at our essence, are natural elements of the Universe. We are an expression of the Universe being conscious of itself. We are not separate from the Universe, despite what the self concept in our head leads us to believe.
- You can cultivate a much deeper appreciation of this truth by paying attention to how the voice in your head operates. Mindfulness meditation is one of the oldest and still the best way of doing this.
- Meditation is the practice of being present and becoming present when we discover we're not.
- Being present is what permeates all the ideas

covered in this book. "Having presence" means being present consistently enough for people to be affected by you.

Coach's assignment

- Begin noticing how the voice of the thoughts in your head shows up every day, in just about every moment. Simply notice it.
- If you've never tried mindfulness meditation, try it. Download an app and do the introductory series. Find a guided meditation on YouTube.
- If you've practiced meditation before, take it one step further. Deepen your practice or lengthen your practice. Sign up for a retreat.

6

TEAR DOWN THE WALL

If you want others to be happy, practice compassion. If you want to be happy, practice compassion.

— DALAI LAMA

There is an old Cherokee legend that goes as follows:

An old man was teaching his grandson about life. "There is a fight that goes on inside all of us," he said. "It is a terrible fight and it is between two wolves. One wolf is evil. He is anger, envy, sorrow, regret, greed, arrogance, self-pity, guilt, resentment, inferiority, lies, false pride, superiority, and ego."

The old man paused for a moment, then continued. "The other wolf is good. He is joy, peace, love, hope, serenity, humility, kindness, benevolence, empathy, generosity, truth, compassion, and faith. That same fight is going on inside of you, my son, and inside every person."

The boy thought about this for a moment. Then he asked his grandfather: "Which wolf wins?"

The old man pondered his grandson's question and said quietly, "The one you feed."

I've heard this story many times and it always moves me. I suppose that's because I've come to recognize its truth in myself. On the surface level, it illustrates what I wrote in the last chapter. Your experience of the world will reflect the thoughts and feelings that you generate from within. On a deeper level, I've experienced personally what it's like to choose one wolf over the other. When I embody the characteristics of the evil wolf, my ego feels energized at first, but over time, it leaves me feeling depleted. When I embrace the characteristics of the good wolf, I am rewarded with feeling more centered, more in control of my emotions, and more alive, probably because it energizes my deeper, more powerful self, instead of my ego.

There is an example of this dynamic that I want to explore in this chapter, a particular embodiment of that evil wolf. I'm talking about your Inner Judge.

Meet your Judge

In Chapter 5, we looked at the way that your thoughts form a voice in your head. When you learn to take notice of that voice, you begin to see that you have different versions of the voice, depending on what circumstances you find yourself in and what types of emotions and thoughts those circumstances elicit in you. One practice that I sometimes use with clients is to personify the voice or voices that you become aware of. Give it a name, describe its features, etc. The point of doing this is that it reinforces the idea from Chapter 5 that *you are not the voice.*

When you become more aware of the voices chattering around in your head, you will eventually discover that one of the most powerful voices is one I call The Judge. Mine is a "he," so I'll use that pronoun. He has nowhere near the power that he used to, but my Judge was once a more powerful presence in my life. As you read this chapter, I want you to ask yourself whether you have met your own Judge yet. I use the word "yet," because I've never met a person who doesn't have an Inner Judge. Some have mastered it more than others, and others might not agree that it needs mastering. Most people are simply unaware of how prevalent their Inner Judge is. Whatever your starting point, open your awareness to the possibility that you're carrying around a Judge, or inner critic, in your head.

Think for a moment of someone who is difficult to work with. *What's wrong with that guy, anyway?* Think for a moment about the dude who cut you off in traffic this morning. *Does that jerk think he's the only one in a hurry?* Or maybe it's the guy in front of you at the grocery checkout counter, insisting that his Metamucil was on sale and making the clerk go check (and then probably writing a paper check for his payment!). Let's make it more personal. Think about your wife, when she tells you for the third time to do the dishes, or think about your husband, when he tells you he's golfing tomorrow, forgetting that you told him about the art festival you really wanted to see with him. Think about your young son, when he took a large red Sharpie pen to your bedroom carpet. If imagining any of these situations provokes a response in you, say hello to your Inner Judge.

Your Inner Judge tells you what's wrong in the world. He can also be the one who tells you what's right in the world, though it's usually by comparing it to what's wrong. Most of us don't like to admit to being "judgmental," but let's just be honest with ourselves right now, okay? The Inner Judge is a near universal characteristic of the human mind. It's the most common expression of the human ego. While everyone has one, not everyone allows it the same amount of power. That is our focus here. Not how do we eliminate the Judge, which is largely a fruitless exercise, but how do we disempower it.

It's very likely that your Judge has you convinced he's necessary. You might be thinking, *"My Inner Judge protects me! Without it, I'd be taken advantage of. If I didn't look at others with a critical eye, I couldn't succeed in the corporate world. I need to be a judge of talent. I need to be able to make the tough calls!"* Do not be fooled by these arguments. They conflate judging a person with being able to discern good and bad behavior.

You can't succeed in the world, especially the corporate world, without being able to make difficult decisions, including ones that won't be popular or that will have a negative impact on others. It's hard to see sometimes, but that is independent from how you feel toward another human being. In other words, the judgment I'm talking about shows up not so much in the *actions* that you take, but in your *way of being* toward the humans involved. I can fire someone with judgment in my heart, or I can fire someone with compassion in my heart. In either case, the action is the same. Your Inner Judge is found less in your specific behavior, than in what you are holding in your heart when you act. You still have the same range of behavioral options—with or without the Judge in your heart.

Now, it is true that holding the Judge in your heart might actually enable some behavior that is more difficult without the Judge. The classic example is the way that soldiers have (for all of modern history at least) demonized and "otherized" their enemy as a coping mechanism for their actions (i.e., killing people). But it's also true that a soldier can fight a war with respect and admiration for his enemy (albeit, while still killing them). You can find examples of this throughout history, from Civil War gentleman officers to the spontaneous "silent night truce" in a trench on the Western Front on December 24, 1914.

Your Inner Judge is not a requirement; he just makes some difficult things easier for you. Fortunately, in the corporate world, we are not killing each other. There are, however, difficult challenges to face, and your Inner Judge likes to show up and make it easier for you to take actions that may hurt other people. You can rein in your Judge by tearing down the wall, which we'll look at next

Tear down the wall

My favorite musical artist of all time is Pink Floyd. One of their most successful albums is called *The Wall*. The essence of the album is about the wall we humans build between each other. The penultimate track on the album is called *The Trial*, and the lyrics in the last verse of the song come from the perspective of, you guessed it, the Judge. In the final line, the Judge says "Since, my friend, you have revealed your deepest fear, I sentence you to be exposed before your peers." Then his voice booms "TEAR DOWN THE WALL!" and the chant from the gallery begins, with the orchestra building toward its crescendo: "Tear down the WALL! Tear down the WALL! Tear down the WALL!"

So, what's the opposite of the wall between people? It starts with empathy, and it goes deeper with intimacy. This is difficult for many leaders. You might be thinking "What place does intimacy have in the corporate world?! Sounds like an HR issue to me." Or you may be thinking that you need to keep a professional distance from those you work with, and in particular, those who work for you. Let me say from the outset, I am not talking about crossing boundaries to inappropriate behavior. It's absolutely critical to define our own boundaries and to respect the boundaries defined by others. The problem is that we unconsciously create boundaries, like the mask in Chapter 3, or the wall we're talking about here, that prevent us from connecting with others.

You are a human being and you have hopes, desires, needs, fears, and challenges. Guess what? So does every other human being. They may not be the same as yours, but they do exist. We forget this when we're focused on our own wants and needs, and we especially forget this when someone else's wants and needs seem to conflict with our own. We get defensive. Our Inner Judge steps in. Our guard goes up and we deal with the other person through our ego.

You can see this show up in the silos and turf battles of corporate life. Engineering assumes Marketing are a bunch of lightweights who don't understand the product. Marketing believes Engineering is out of touch with the reality of what matters to our customers. The Field thinks Corporate HQ likes to dream up processes that do nothing but hurt our business. Corporate HQ thinks the Field are a bunch of cowboys, flaunting our processes and controls. We get so wrapped up in the apparent conflicts between us and them that we forget they are human beings, just like us, and they probably just want the same things as we do. We create a wall in the relationship—and the empathy and intimacy required to productively collaborate and overcome conflict gets lost.

Into me see

A leadership teacher of mine described intimacy as "into me see." What I'm talking about here is seeing and being seen. When I talk to my clients about connecting with others, there is often the misunderstanding that I mean get to know stuff about their lives, like what they did this weekend, what their family is like, and what they want in their career. Those are certainly elements of connection, but I'm really talking about intimate connection: two people seeing each other, understanding each other, while respecting boundaries of course.

On a recent road trip, I walked into a gas station in the middle of nowhere and immediately noticed the grumpy clerk working the counter. She was scowling and making annoyed remarks to her co-worker. She was missing some teeth, had the voice of a 40-year smoker, and appeared not to have been taking very good care of herself. She was somebody my well-developed Inner Judge likes to have a field day with. But I've grown, so when I was ready to pay for my snacks, I looked her in the eye, smiled warmly, and said "Rough day, huh?" She held my eyes for just an instant and I saw her face soften. She smiled back and said

"Nah, I'm just playin'." I walked out and never saw her again, yet I would describe what happened as an intimate connection. I might never have seen past the idea I had in my mind of a rude gas station attendant mad at life, and she might never have seen me as more than a city slicker who thinks he's better than everyone else. Instead, we dropped our guards and caught a glimpse of each other, however briefly.

Similarly, imagine you are walking through the woods on a beautiful day. The sun is shining, the temperature is perfect, and you're feeling fine. You round the corner and there in front of you, no more than about 15 feet away, is a fox. Both of you freeze. He sees you and you see him. He knows you see him and you know he sees you. After what seems like an eternity, he breaks contact and bounds into the trees. That, too, is an intimate connection. Why do you think it's difficult to hold eye contact with people? Eye contact alone creates an intimate connection.

This is something you can practice. Come out of your own head and make intimate connections wherever you can. Be present enough to see other people and to let them see you. Talk to the stranger waiting in line with you at the grocery store. Flirt with your waiter. Go see the colleague you've been emailing back and forth and really listen to what they're saying. Open an honest conversation with your counterpart in the department you keep clashing with. See the humanity in others, in all of its flaws and beauty. The reason to practice this is so you can experience its power. Intimate connection transforms the moment. It has an impact on all parties involved, which makes it critical to influencing others, but more importantly, it changes you. It silences your Inner Judge. It teaches you to recognize your impact. And it feels good.

Accept people the way they are

To disempower your Inner Judge is simply to accept people—as they are. This is not the same thing as accepting their behavior, or accepting their ideas, or accepting any kind of mistreatment. In fact, to accept someone—unconditionally, as a human—empowers you to more effectively challenge their behavior.

If I see another executive as the obstacle between me and what I want, I'm more likely to approach them in a way that just makes them defensive, saying something like "Why do you keep undermining my proposal?" Or maybe I don't even bother approaching them, because why would I? They don't care about my needs or they'd already be supporting my proposal! On the other hand, if my starting place toward my colleague is one of curiosity and understanding that they have their own wants and needs, then I am better able to approach them about their behavior without making it personal, and without making them feel attacked. I might instead say "I appreciate that you took the time to share your concerns about my proposal. I'd like to better understand your concerns. Can we spend a few minutes talking about it?" The latter approach doesn't put them on the defensive, and they feel more safe to engage in a conversation with real dialogue.

The power of compassionate acceptance

When you accept someone compassionately, you are changed. I'm not arguing that you should adopt this approach because it's the morally right thing to do, though that argument is pretty compelling, and in my opinion correct. I'm telling you to be compassionate with your fellow humans because *it transforms you*. You will experience this transformation in two ways.

First, like the client I described in Chapter 4, you will feel like a heavy burden has been lifted from your shoulders. It's emotionally and even physically draining to carry around judgment toward others. It saps your energy. This is true at the neurological level. Your Inner Judge is identifying threats, which creates tension and anxiety (i.e., the stress response). That stress response is a physical response, in the form of cortisol pumping into your body, your muscles tensing, and your heart rate elevating. That can initially feel energizing, because your body is preparing you to handle the threat (i.e., fight or flight), but it will always leave you feeling depleted in the long run.

Compassion, on the other hand, activates a different system in your brain, releasing the neurotransmitter oxytocin. Oxytocin creates an effect that is the opposite of stress, which is a sense of contentment and well-being. Compassion puts you in a state of being that is far more energizing and empowering in the long run.

The second part of the transformation you'll experience is that you'll discover you have a far different impact on people. You will experience less defensiveness from others. You'll find that people are more willing to be open and honest with you. People will respond more positively to you, plain and simple. This is something tangible you can feel—if you pay attention.

Practicing compassion and accepting others as they are will liberate you from the fears that your Inner Judge tries to keep alive. Rather than the ups and downs of repeatedly getting triggered by other people's behavior, you'll carry yourself with more equanimity and inner calm. From this liberated state, you can more confidently and more effectively address the challenges you face with other people.

So much of Corporate Hell is dealing with daily frustrations about other people's behavior. It's the kind of environment where your Inner Judge can run amok, without you even realizing it's happening, and without realizing that you can do something about it.

Imagine what it would be like to disempower that Judge. Rather than other people being sources of Corporate Hell, they are simply fellow travelers, making their way through life, the same as you. Connecting with others through empathy and compassion energizes you. It gives you a better place to relate to people from. It gives you a better place to lead from.

Chapter summary

- A major voice we all carry in our head is the Inner Judge.
- Judging people is not the same as discerning between good and bad behavior or evaluating the merits of a decision or given situation.
- Judgment toward others creates a wall between people.
- Empathy is understanding other people without judgment. It does not require condoning or agreeing with people's behavior.
- Intimacy is what's created when two people see each other empathetically.
- Accepting another person compassionately, for who they are, separate from their behavior or choices, opens the door for empathy and intimacy.
- Dropping the Judge and connecting with empathy and intimacy removes the wall between people. From here, conflict can be resolved in a constructive way, and problems can be solved in a collaborative way.

Coach's assignment

- Put yourself in the shoes of a colleague with whom you are having a conflict. Schedule a meeting with that colleague and go into it with only one goal—to understand their perspective. Put your own agenda aside and just listen.
- Make an intimate connection with a stranger, even if it's just smiling and saying hello. Notice the impact it has on the other person. Notice what impact it has on you.

PART III

TAKE RESPONSIBILITY

In Part 1, we focused on you and how you show up. The focus of our attention was on your inner experience. In Part 2, we expanded our attention outward to encompass how you connect, not just with yourself, but with others. In Part 3, we'll build on that foundation and you'll expand your attention even further to the world around you. In these last three chapters, we'll explore how you can take responsibility as a leader in your world.

7

ACCEPT WHAT IS

When you argue with reality, you lose—but only 100% of the time.

— BYRON KATIE

Remember the boss I described in the opening pages of this book? Let's call her "Amy" and I'll tell you now why I got sideways with her. She was a very talented, smart executive, and for about a year, we got along great. But she was also incredibly ambitious, making most of the work we did together all about making her look good to her boss and our CEO. And she was competitive. Not in the healthy way, but in the political way, where it's a zero-sum game.

I worked very closely with one of her peers, someone she frequently had conflicts with. Let's call him "Paul." I personally listened to Amy throw Paul under the bus on numerous occasions with our CEO, while Paul was not around. In fact, she was gunning for his job, and Paul made it easy for her with his own mis-steps, so Amy was eventually successful in helping him out the door. A few months later, Amy was named his replacement, and several months after that, she managed to get herself fired, but that's not the story I want to tell you right now. That's just karma finally catching up.

Before all that happened, my job required me to travel with Paul frequently. Whenever Amy would have a conflict with Paul, she would blame me for not intervening before it happened, or for not warning her about what Paul was thinking. One day, Amy's assistant walked into my office and informed me I was to accompany Paul on every trip related to our project, something that had not been necessary before. In short, I was meant to spy on Paul and report back to Amy.

Then one Saturday, after I had been on the road with Paul all week, Paul attacked Amy over email about something he was unhappy about. Amy was furious with me for not warning her Paul was going to do this. I was on a Cub Scout camping trip with my son and I started getting text messages from my assistant saying "Amy wants to know where you are and why you're not intervening in this conflict she's having. She expects you to see her about this first thing Monday morning." The next night is when she sent me the email I referred to at the start of this book.

This particular event was the culmination of several

months of similar clashes. During that time, I was absolutely miserable. I felt like none of it was fair. I felt like I shouldn't have to deal with such a terrible boss. I felt like she was to blame for how unhappy I was. If only I didn't have to deal with this situation, I would be so much happier. In other words, *I felt like my corporate life was hell because of the circumstances I found myself in.*

So, was my boss the reason for my Corporate Hell, or was it all the energy I was putting into being frustrated over the way things were, wishing they were different?

Stop resisting

The number one impediment to taking responsibility for difficult situations is an overpowering resistance to accept the situation in the first place. How often do you find yourself thinking *I wish things were different. I wish my boss wasn't such a jerk. I wish they would recognize my contributions and give me a raise. I wish my husband would stop watching football all day and mow the damn lawn* and so on?

We resist reality when we wish things were different. That feeling inside is **resistance**. You might believe that it's a good thing, because after all, doesn't taking responsibility begin with wanting a different reality? No, it does not *start* there. Taking responsibility must always begin with accepting the way things are. That doesn't preclude taking leadership action to change things; it just defines your starting point. Otherwise, you're simply getting in your own way.

What does the resistance I'm talking about look like in practice? Well, for starters, it's those "I wish" thoughts. Wishing things away never created change, but it's a juicy activity for the voice in your head to engage in. It's a short jump from wishing to complaining to blaming. And what does blaming get you, honestly? Nothing but misery. It's just fuel for your Inner Judge. It feeds the evil wolf and blocks constructive action. Blaming others for what's wrong makes it easy to avoid taking responsibility. Taking responsibility does *not* mean taking the blame, nor does it preclude holding others accountable for their behavior. It just means choosing to respond in a constructive way to your current reality.

Instead of blaming, start by accepting *what is*. Stop resisting. Accept what is, knowing that it doesn't preclude what could be. It's just our starting point. It's a *way of being in relation* to our circumstances. You can be in a state of *resistance* to what is, or you can be in a state of *acceptance* of what is. Neither one changes what is, but only the latter positions you to *do something constructive* about what is. It's difficult to respond from a place of wishing things were different because the focus is on what's wrong and all the reasons things are not as you'd like them to be. You find yourself starting a lot of sentences with "if only…". *If only I had more money. If only my boss were more enlightened. If only my team could understand and do what I want.* Accepting what is, on the other hand, eliminates the "if only" excuse. Now you're free to respond to the current reality.

Question reality

Let's go even deeper with this. If we're accepting what is, we need to be much better at actually knowing *what is true*. I want you to stop resisting reality, but I also want you to question reality. That may sound paradoxical, so bear with me. I've already told you that much of what you perceive to be reality is made up in your head. This is where you need to put that insight to good use.

We are assumption-making machines. You make assumptions so pervasively that you probably don't even realize how much you do it. Imagine this scenario: in the staff meeting this morning, the boss shot down your idea in front of everyone. Is that a true statement of "what is?" How many assumptions or made-up elements do you think we can pull out of this? There are two right on the surface: that the idea was "shot down" and that everyone was paying attention. These surface assumptions might end up being accurate, but it's important to see that you've made an assumption. More importantly, you need to examine the assumptions under the surface, where the deeper you go, the more unlikely the chance that it's accurate.

Believing the idea was shot down is full of assumptions about your boss's intentions. In addition to assuming they *intended* to shoot it down, there's the assumption that it was because they didn't like your idea. Or maybe that they're too afraid to take a risk. Or maybe they're too stupid to see the value of your idea. Maybe you assumed you are deficient in some way because you can't sell your ideas effectively, or can't come up with good ideas in the first place. You might assume that because it was in front of everyone, your peers are judging you, and that they agree the idea was bad. Maybe you assume your peers are laughing inside at your misfortune, or feeling sorry for you having to deal with the idiot we all call our manager. Possibly, you're assuming they shot down your idea because you're a woman or because you're a man, or because you're too young and inexperienced to have good ideas, or because you're too old and stuck in the past.

How many of those assumptions are likely to be true? For every assumption you claim is true, ask yourself: *how do I know it's true?* If you do this honestly, you will soon discover how many assumptions you make without stopping to think about it. In this example, what's true is that the person designated as your manager said some words and displayed some visual body language after you presented your idea. Immediately following that, your idea was no longer discussed in the meeting. Everything else, *even if it's true*, is just an assumption, unless and until you've taken further action to test the assumption.

This is how we operate, and frankly, we couldn't survive 10 minutes in this world if we didn't do that. Our brains fill in the meaning of everything that happens to us; otherwise we'd be overwhelmed with stimuli we couldn't make sense of. We create meaning in a subjective way, largely through our assumptions, conclusions, and opinions, etc.

Manage your assumptions

I'm not suggesting you try to stop making assumptions. I'm saying you can make this human tendency serve you rather than work against you. You do this in two steps. First, you relentlessly practice uncovering your assumptions. The better you get at this, the more surprised you'll be at what you've been doing to yourself. One of the most useful things I do as a coach for my clients is question their assumptions. All the time I ask, "How do you know that? What leads you to believe it?" You can imagine how that usually goes. Often, the first answer is "I don't know, I just know." When they begin offering explanations, then additional assumptions start tumbling out, and they soon discover how deeply their assumption-making goes.

Start asking yourself these questions when you find yourself frustrated and telling stories in your head:

- How do I know that?
- Is it true?
- How do I know it's true?
- What assumptions am I making?

Second, practice the art of changing your assumptions. This is only really possible if you've done step one. You can't change your assumptions if you don't understand that you're making them in the first place. Take our example and tell me whether any of these assumptions are more or less likely to be true than the ones I came up with earlier:

- *My boss is stressed about his job and is not slowing down enough to listen.*
- *I didn't explain my idea as well as I know I could have.*
- *My boss is fearful of trusting his reputation to my idea and he probably needs my help to build better trust between us.*
- *My boss didn't see the value in my idea, but that has nothing to do with me, my abilities, or the value of the idea.*

These are still assumptions, but they have a different impact on me. They put me in a more constructive place from which to act. If I haven't taken it personally, I'm not defensive, and if I'm not defensive, I can take more effective action. That's the whole point here. By questioning and even changing our own assumptions, we increase our ability to respond effectively to difficult events when they happen.

Assume positive intent

I do a lot of Team Coaching with leadership teams and other types of corporate teams. One thing we do is develop agreements for working together that the team commits to keeping. Almost always, we end up with an agreement called "Assume positive intent." Why? Because teams that talk with each other openly, like they do in my Team Coaching sessions, quickly discover how much they assume, often incorrectly, about other people's intentions. Many of the problems they face come from assuming the worst about other people's intentions, and that's usually wrong. Simply agreeing to always assume positive intent changes the dynamic and helps the team deal with conflict constructively.

People don't usually set out with bad intent toward their co-workers. Everyone has their own needs and wants, and when those needs and wants conflict with my own needs and wants, it's easy to assume bad intent on their part. Instead, I can empathize with the other person's perspective and assume positive intent as my starting point.

Embrace your "response-ability"

If I start with seeing reality more clearly, unencumbered by all my automatic assumptions, I can begin to address difficult situations in a much more constructive and creative way. I can choose new follow-up actions to test my assumptions. I can assume positive intent, making useful assumptions that motivate me and don't make me defensive. By doing this, I'm taking control of my own response. I'm building my ability to respond in a way that serves me. I call this my "response-ability."

Viktor Frankl wrote extensively about this, as I mentioned in Chapter 2. He discovered this ability in the worst imaginable circumstances, surviving a Nazi German concentration camp. Anyone can be forgiven for giving up under such circumstances, where all freedom appears lost. What Frankl discovered is that even under such circumstances, there are freedoms that can never be taken away —as long as you have the strength to hold on to them. Chief among these freedoms is the power to choose your response, especially your inner response.

When he returned to his life in Austria, he founded a new field of psychotherapy called "logotherapy," based on the Greek word "λόγος" ("logos," which translates as "reason" or "meaning"). The basic premise of this approach is that not only can you choose your response in any situation, you can also choose to define the meaning of the events that happen in your life.

Embracing your response-ability includes defining your own meaning for life's events, and then choosing your own meaningful response. This is **liberation**. I don't claim that circumstances won't at times be incredibly difficult, but I do claim that you can free yourself from feeling dependent on circumstances. No longer do you need to wish for things to be different before you can get what you want. Paradoxically, if you accept what is, you are better equipped to actually change what is.

When I was given the choice that morning by my former boss, the response I chose was to leave the situation. I chose to quit my job and start a new career that I had always dreamed I might someday do. But what if I had chosen to stay? What if my dream job was continuing to do what I was doing for the company I was doing it for? What's possible if I accept what is and embrace my response-ability?

The answer is that I can be much more creative. When I speak in hindsight about the difficulty I experienced with my former boss, I feel absolutely certain that it was good for me. It forced me to face many of my own issues and I grew from the experience. I feel fortunate that circumstances gave me an opportunity to create something new for myself. Imagine if I had that clarity of perspective earlier. Rather than being miserable, bemoaning my misfortune at having to deal with Corporate Hell, I could have seen it for what it was: an opportunity. It was an opportunity to create change all along; I just didn't seize the opportunity until circumstances forced me to.

You will inevitably face challenging circumstances, so in the next chapter, we'll explore what it means to see challenges as an opportunity to create change.

Chapter summary

- When we wish circumstances were different, we are resisting reality.
- We also obscure reality with our unconscious assumptions.
- Improving our ability to see what assumptions we're making gives us the ability to be more intentional with those assumptions. We can choose assumptions that serve us, rather than hinder us.
- Assuming positive intent is one of the most powerful changes we can make.
- Accepting what is and managing our assumptions improves our ability to respond creatively and constructively. This is response-ability.

Coach's assignment

- Reflect on this question: What reality are you resisting in your life today?
- Every time you make a judgment about a person or draw a conclusion about someone's motivations, ask yourself: Is it true? How do I know it's true? What else could be true?

8

—————

CREATE CHANGE

To hell with circumstances; I create opportunities.

— BRUCE LEE

The well-known phrase "when life gives you lemons, make lemonade" has become almost a cliché, but the spirit behind it is important. History is full of examples of people who—in the midst of great adversity—accomplished amazing things. Nelson Mandela spent 27 years in prison before being released to lead South Africa out of apartheid. Oprah Winfrey suffered terribly at the hands of others when she was growing up, yet still emerged to become one of the most powerful figures in the history of entertainment. Richard Branson had dyslexia and did poorly in school. Franklin Roosevelt had polio, and Jim Carrey was homeless. And

I've already pointed out the impact on the world that Viktor Frankl made after suffering in a Nazi concentration camp.

In my own life, I am grateful for some of the challenges I've had to face. If I hadn't faced my own Corporate Hell, I may never have transcended it and changed my career to one of helping others do the same. I could have gone in the opposite direction, burrowing deeper behind the mask, growing more distant from any sense of life purpose, and disconnecting from the people and resources I had available to me. Instead, I reinvented myself. I created a new career for myself. I wrote a book about it and began speaking in public about *feelings* and *the Universe*, something I couldn't have imagined myself doing 10 years ago.

I chose to lead my life instead of follow my fears. I chose to create from what life gave me, rather than be a victim of its difficulties.

You are not a victim

It's easy to feel like a victim in corporate life. There is so much you don't control. You don't control how much you're paid. You don't control whom you report to. You don't control when you get the promotion, whether you get a raise, or how much of a bonus you get. Often, you don't even have control over what work you're expected to complete. In many cases, you don't control what time you start and end your day, whether or not you can work remotely, or when you can take a vacation. These are among the many things that can make corporate life feel like hell.

When I use the term "victim" with my clients, they often react defensively. Nobody likes to see themselves as a victim, but whenever we blame our difficulties on circumstances we don't control, we are, by definition, being a victim of our circumstances. This is completely understandable, though the point of this book is to show you how it doesn't need to be that way. By now, you've discovered a different way of responding and you've tapped into a much deeper well of personal power. You have the power to choose, which at its core is the power to *create*. You can choose your response, which means you can choose your mindset, and a creative mindset is far more powerful than a victim mindset.

What does that mean exactly? Do you see setbacks as obstacles, preventing you from achieving your goals? Or do you see them as opportunities? Let's say you put together a very well-constructed presentation for a strategic initiative. During the presentation, the executives in the room ask some tough questions, pointing out potential flaws in your thinking, and at the end, the CEO thanks you and sends you back to the drawing board. I've been that presenter on a few occasions, and I've been sitting among the skeptical executives on many more occasions.

Those experiences allowed me to see the two different

responses in action. In one response, the presenter sees those tough questions as an attack on their idea, takes it personally, and concludes that the other people in the room are obstacles blocking their progress. This response feels incredibly frustrating. Other people, who don't understand the situation as well as you do, are getting in the way of your idea. You don't have the power to over-rule the decision, so you get angry, and maybe complain to your peers that the Leadership Team doesn't get it. In the process, you become less present to the actual reality— starting in the meeting when the executives were questioning your idea, and continuing on for hours or days afterward, as you stew on their lack of understanding.

Alternatively, you can stay present—and learn from what's happening. Rather than taking the tough questions personally, which causes an internal emotional reaction, you could engage them more openly, without defensiveness. In doing so, you might actually learn something from the exchange, like how your critical stakeholders think. You might even change the dynamics of the situation. When you are defensive to criticism, especially in a situation like presenting to a leadership team of which you are not a member, things can quickly turn ugly, encouraging others to pile on. On the other hand, if you engage openly and confidently, but without defensiveness, you can generate dialogue. A creative response to a tough question might be: "You're raising a valid point that my team and I have wrestled with. What we've learned is that..." Or maybe you could respond with another question: "Before I react, I want to be sure I understand your point. Can you say a little more about what your concern is?"

In this way, the tough questions can be an opportunity to educate the leadership team, or even *learn from* the leadership team. If there is validity in the tough questions, you'll be more open to hearing the message and incorporating the feedback as appropriate. If the questions are uninformed, you've been given the opportunity to inform a key stakeholder. Either way, you've changed the dynamic and gotten more open dialogue to happen, which is critical in actually getting to the best outcome.

Every single moment is an opportunity to be creative with your response, rather than a victim of circumstances. Responding creatively allows you to have a different impact, enabling you to influence the direction that events are flowing—if only you stay present to the opportunity.

Be a creator

Life gets messy. People screw up. You'll be misunderstood or treated unfairly. Setbacks will happen. These are not bugs in the system—they are features of a human world. If you let yourself feel like a victim of those features, you miss the chance to be a creator.

There was a night several years ago when I was sitting in a hotel room, depressed, feeling like my marriage was not going to survive. Like most couples, my wife and I had discovered how much work it takes to make a marriage thrive for the long haul, and now we were facing some pretty difficult circumstances. That night, a friend of mine recommended a book called *The Power of TED* (*The Empowerment Dynamic)* by David Emerald. In this short book, I learned how easily we slip into a victim mindset, where we feel persecuted and need rescuing. David calls this "the Dreaded Drama Triangle," where the sufferer sees every situation as a drama with a ***victim***, ***persecutor***, or potential ***rescuer***. The Empowerment Dynamic is a switch of those roles to be a ***creator*** (rather than victim), ***challenger*** (rather than persecutor), or ***coach*** (rather than rescuer). The facts of the situation may be the same, but one perspective is empowering (creator) while the other is disempowering (victim).

My wife taught me the power of being a creator in the weeks to come, as we worked together to reconnect and ultimately get to where we are today, which is stronger than we ever were before. The circumstances that led us there could have been disempowering, but instead, they empowered us to create change.

In the presentation example, the presenter may see themselves as a victim being persecuted by the others, looking for someone else in the room to step up and rescue them. Their own boss may be sitting in the room and feel the need to step into the role of rescuer. The Empowerment Dynamic flips the script, putting the presenter in the role of a creator engaging with challengers. Rather than trying to be the rescuer, the boss can lead from behind and coach the presenter, either before or after the meeting, or even during the meeting—with a well-timed question that leads the presenter to perform at their best.

Because managers are accountable for the success of their teams, it's common for managers to step into that rescuer role, trying to make sure their people don't fail. However, this takes the ownership away from people, which can make them feel like a victim. Even though the manager's intent is good (to help the employee), the impact is disempowering. Instead, the manager who learns to coach and support is able to help their employee be more of a creator.

Managers who target an employee they feel is not living up to performance expectations can inadvertently slip into the role of persecutor, at least in the eyes of the employee, who then obligingly takes on the role of victim. If that manager instead learns to confront poor performance in a direct and honest, yet constructive and compassionate way, then they can serve as a challenger, helping the employee be more of a creator than a victim.

In all of these scenarios, you have the opportunity to choose The Empowerment Dynamic, rather than the Dreaded Drama Triangle, to use David Emerald's language. The really important point is that it's not dependent on circumstances. It's just a fundamentally different way of responding to any circumstances you find yourself in, particularly difficult circumstances.

Plant your stake and create your response

To respond creatively requires that you have something orienting you toward what you want to create. We'll call this your **stake**. Earlier, we defined "leadership" as the choice to take responsibility for your world—and the way we represent such choices is in the form of stakes. When you're living life on purpose (which we covered in Chapter 2), you metaphorically *plant a stake in the ground* every time you choose to take responsibility within a given set of circumstances. To intentionally create change in the world, you need to hold a stake.

A stake always has context. The context can be very small, such as a one-hour meeting, or it can be very large, such as the world. You could hold a stake that says *in this meeting, all opinions will be respectfully heard*, and you could hold a stake that says *no one in the world should go hungry*. Your stake is defined by the scope in which you seek to create change.

A stake is not a goal or an outcome, but goals and outcomes can serve your stake. Goals are measurable and specific. They are designed as milestones toward something bigger and are important tools of management. Stakes, on the other hand, are tools of leadership. A stake is an articulation of what you *want* and it serves to guide your behavior. The best way to articulate a stake is to ask yourself "What do I truly want?" in a given situation or context.

Just like a stake in the ground, your leadership stake serves as an anchoring point, keeping you present to what you truly want. Your stake is at the center of your ability to respond creatively, or what I referred to at the end of Chapter 7 as your "response-ability." Let's take a look at what a practical model of "response-ability looks like.

Practice the leadership response-ability cycle

You are faced every moment with the opportunity to respond creatively. You respond to the vast majority of moments automatically, through habits and unconscious motives. Your ability to respond consciously and creatively—rather than automatically—is where your leadership power lies. This process functions in a cyclical way. You are faced with a version of reality, you respond, you have some kind of impact, you are faced with a new version of reality, you respond, and on it goes.

The key to making this process *conscious*, rather than automatic, is to be clear about your ***stake*** in every situation. You can imagine planting your stake in the center of a given situation or scenario. Circling around your stake are three dynamic elements:

- An ***awareness*** of what's happening, relative to your stake. This requires you to listen, watch, and suspend assumptions.

- The ***response*** you choose in service of the stake. This is where you *do* or *say* something.
- The ***impact*** that's made with your response. You are always having an impact. This is about paying closer attention to what that impact is, especially relative to your original stake.

Permeating it all is ***presence***, which is a necessary ingredient for all the other elements to be effective. Shown graphically, these elements look like this:

I'll give you a simple example of how this might look in practice. Let's say you're a product marketing manager and your stake for an upcoming product launch is to change the way people think about your industry. In support of this stake, you develop a compelling and innovative go-to-market strategy ("response" in the model). When you present the strategy to your boss and peers, the reception is lukewarm. You become aware of a change of energy in the room. You notice some people shifting in their chairs and a few people exchanging glances, then your boss says that the risks of such a radical approach are not worth taking. The impact you're having is to make people uncomfortable, which creates resistance to your idea. It's not the impact you were expecting or hoping for, but it is the impact you're having.

This is a crucial point in the model. Upon noticing your impact, how do you respond? A common response is *fight or flight*. You either press harder, fighting to defend your point of view, or you get frustrated and give up, concluding that these people are standing in your way. Either way, in terms of our model, you would be abandoning your stake. It's easy to see how giving up is abandoning your stake, but maybe you're wondering how defending your point of view is abandoning it? In defending your point of view, you've let go of your stake (i.e., to change the way people think about your industry) and grabbed something else—the need to be right. Think about it. In order to be right about your strategy, you need your boss and peers to be wrong about their concerns. Your behavior is now guided more by your need to prove yourself right than by your true stake.

A more constructive response, which is consistent with the model presented here, is to stay present to the impact you're having—or *become* present again if necessary. Continue to focus your awareness on what's needed from you in order to move toward your leadership stake. In this case, the impact you might notice is that people get uncomfortable, your peers display certain body language, and your boss expresses his concerns about the risks involved. Staying present allows you to see this for the absolutely perfect opportunity that it is. Your boss and peers may be just like those people in the market whose perception of your industry you seek to change. Their response is your first indication that you might be on to something—that you are truly challenging the status quo of your industry.

By staying present, you see the opportunity to create from the impact you had. Rather than fight or give up, you can *engage*. You can follow your curiosity and learn more about the concerns raised by your boss and peers. By understanding and *empathizing* with their concerns, you can adjust the way you present your strategy. Most importantly, you keep yourself in the game, ready to respond again in service of your stake.

At the next opportunity, you present your strategy again, but in a way that more empathetically meets the audience where they are. You stay present and notice a different impact, and you continue to respond and act—in a cyclical way—in support of your stake. The key is that you stay present to your stake, are aware of your impact relative to your stake, and are ready to act again.

Do, be, do, be, do

This is not a linear and orderly process. You're constantly making adjustments in your response to bring your impact in closer alignment with your stake. I like to think of this model like a game of tetherball from your childhood playground days. In tetherball, you have a ball tethered to a post with a chain, and the goal is to knock that ball around the post until the chain wraps itself around the post. The post is like your stake and the ball represents your opportunity to respond. Success in tetherball comes from patiently focusing your awareness on the ball, striking at it when the opportunity arises, seeing what impact your strike has on the ball, and staying present for another chance to strike at it. The key is timing. It's an alternating pattern of do (i.e., strike the ball), be (i.e., wait and watch carefully for the moment to hit the ball again), do (i.e., strike the ball again), be (notice your impact), and around it goes. Do be do be do.

Leadership is the same. While I've broken apart the process in this model, in practice it's much more fluid and intuitive. The responding part is not the hard part. You likely already do this. Being action-oriented is what's expected of you in the corporate world and you've become good at it. The core of this model is bringing presence and awareness of your impact into the process. The first two parts of this book, and in particular Chapter 5, were about how to do that. This model is a way of reminding you that *doing* is only half the equation. Putting the two together—*being and doing*—is how you become the creator of change in your world. After all, we don't call ourselves "human doings."

You create change by doing and by being. You create out of the circumstances of your life. Every moment, whatever is happening in that moment, is an opportunity to create. When something frustrating or difficult happens, you create from that. You never create change in a vacuum— you always create change from what you're given. Everything is material to create from. I won't say the world is a hard place—I will say the world is a challenging place, giving you infinite opportunities to create your own response.

Whether you're a front-line employee or a CEO, the implication is the same. You create change, on whatever scale makes sense for you, by *leading*. Liberate the leader within you by showing up, authentically, with purpose, and with courage. Connect with your world and the people you lead, and take responsibility for creating change. Stop being a victim of Corporate Hell and start creating the change necessary, in yourself and the world around you, to make corporate life the rewarding, fulfilling place it should be.

Chapter Summary

- Corporate life, like life in general, is full of circumstances that are hard and don't seem fair.
- Because so much is beyond your control, it's easy to feel like a victim of circumstances.
- The opposite of a victim mindset is a creator mindset. Rather than feel like a victim of circumstances, you can be the creator of your response to any set of circumstances.
- Embodying the creator mindset requires being present and being intentional in your response.
- The response-ability cycle begins with a clear leadership stake, surrounded by a continuous cycle of awareness, response, and impact. Woven throughout the cycle is presence.
- The power of the response-ability cycle is that it balances *action* with a *way of being*. In leadership, *being* is equal in importance to *doing*.

Coach's assignment

- Create a change in your corporate life. Identify a situation where you are dissatisfied, or not getting the result you want. Take response-ability for creating a change, keeping the follow steps in mind:

1. Clarify your stake. Write it down and carry it with you.
2. Be present and aware for the opportunity to act in service of your stake. When you see it (or hear it, or feel it), act immediately.
3. Be present and curious about your impact.
4. Stay aware to spot the next opportunity to act. Pay attention to ensure you haven't let go of your stake and slipped into the need to be right instead.

- Continue your practice of being—and becoming—present. Take your mindfulness practice to another level.

9

LIBERATE YOURSELF

Change happens when the pain of holding on becomes greater than the fear of letting go.

— Spencer Johnson

E arly on in my coach training, I was working with a master coach, and we were practicing the art of coaching "life purpose." The foundation of a fulfilled life is a sense of purpose, and capturing its essence in a life purpose statement (as we did in Chapter 2) is an important step. Such a statement is typically a simple metaphor and serves as a reminder to its owner of the deeper meaning of the life they are living. It gives them a way of considering the question: *Am I living life on purpose?*

In this practice session with my coach, I came up with my first life purpose statement, or at least the first one I thought of consciously and wrote down. My first life purpose statement was: *I am the liberator, who frees people to live life consciously.* At the time, I was waking up to a more powerful way of being, and the experience for me was one of liberation. It seemed perfectly natural to me that what I was meant to do was help others do the same. Although I have evolved the words a bit, my purpose today remains essentially the same. Today I describe it like this: *I am the dancing light, who liberates humanity with courage, purpose, and love.* The dancing light describes my personality and energy when I'm at my best. I'm not always at my best, but this metaphor serves to remind me of the impact I have when I am. Courage, purpose, and love are what bring out my best self. When I'm at my best, I am liberated from the fear and lack of purpose that usually hold me back. That's when my humanity shines through, and it's my purpose to lead life in this liberated way, while helping others to do the same.

It gives me a sense of direction. It guides me when I think about whether the work I'm doing with my life matters, whether I'm making a difference in the world. I don't live a perfect life and I fall short of my best self all the time, but my life purpose statement sustains me. Liberation began for me by discovering how much I had been living safely in my comfort zone, meeting other people's expectations. It deepened when I created clarity in my life's purpose and chose to be a leader in service of that purpose.

Your purpose is not the same as mine. Your life is not my life. However, by reading this book, you've shown a recognition that even talented, successful people can become frustrated and disillusioned in corporate life. That feeling can be a drain on your soul because it feels like being trapped in a situation you can't change—in Corporate Hell. *But you are not trapped.* My aim with this book has been to inspire you to undertake your own liberation. By sharing my experiences, I hope to show you that if I can do it, surely you can too. However, it's up to you now. It's time for you to liberate the leader within you and be happy in your career.

How badly do you want it?

This is not a quick fix book. I believe I've laid out a formula for liberating the leader within you and being happy at work, but it's not a set of steps that if you just execute them, then corporate life will be bliss. It's a journey, not a destination. I have personally worked on every idea in this book and will continue to do so for the rest of my life. That doesn't mean the destination will always be out of reach. It means the place to be is on the path.

What is it that puts you on the path? Simple. All you have to do is *want it*. If you truly want it, you will embrace these ideas and work on them, in your own way and in your own time. You will grow, you will stumble, and you will grow some more. You will keep learning. You will change, but I like to describe that as becoming *more of who you truly are*. Occasionally, I have a client who is fearful of change. They don't want to let go of who they are. What I tell them is that they are not letting go of who they are. They are letting go of what obscures who they truly are. They are amplifying and uncovering the greatness that lies within. All you have to do to start is want it badly enough.

Corporate decision makers often ask me "What makes a coaching engagement successful?" The answer is simple. Personal and professional growth is a dynamic process, with a lot of contributing variables, but I can sum up my simple answer in one statement: it all depends on how much my client wants it. The status quo is strong, and even someone who wants to develop will struggle against that status quo. But the person who's not interested or not quite ready yet will not grow, no matter what. It's the most fundamental factor in the success of professional growth. Sometimes, it takes a trauma or negative experience to kick-start that desire. Sometimes, it's just the accumulation of several years of tolerating a less than satisfying life that triggers the desire. Some people never lost that desire in the first place, because after all, we all had it at birth. Have you ever seen a toddler who lacked the desire to walk? No matter where it comes from, the desire to grow must be the first ingredient. The fact that you've read this far means you have that desire in you.

Liberate yourself from what?

Corporate Hell is not a place; it's a state of mind. It's the feeling on Sunday night of not wanting to go back to the office tomorrow. It's the feeling of lying awake at night, worrying about the drama going on at work. Corporate Hell is the cynicism and feeling of helplessness in the face of circumstances you cannot control. I hope you've figured out by now that I'm not talking about liberating yourself from difficult circumstances.

We've talked about several human tendencies that serve to shackle us. The safety of hiding behind a mask. The feeling of being lost and living and working without purpose. The isolation of being disconnected, from yourself, the world, and others. And the biggest one of all, the tendency to live one's life from a place of fear more than love. The liberation that I speak of is the liberation from all of those. It's not the absence of those tendencies, but rather the freedom to not be controlled by them. To embrace that freedom, to transcend your own self-imposed limitations, that is to be a liberated leader. From that place, you can choose to stay in a situation or leave a situation, because you are not dependent upon circumstances for your mental and emotional well-being. You are already free.

There are a lot of books out there about how to leave the corporate world and make a living on your own. I'm aware that you may have picked up this book hoping to read about how to escape Corporate Hell, only to have me preach to you about taking responsibility for your own experience. As it happens, taking responsibility for your experience could include leaving a set of circumstances. You wouldn't stay in an abusive situation and tell yourself you should just be a stronger leader. In that situation, the action you take may very well be to leave the situation, but don't take that to be the liberation I'm talking about here.

Lead a liberated life

The liberation we've been talking about throughout this book is one that originates from within. You don't have to stay in Corporate Hell, but you do have to take responsibility for liberating yourself from it. Liberation starts with **showing up** differently than you may have been. You must *choose* to be a leader, whether it's in your job description or not. That doesn't mean you have to become a different person. On the contrary, it means discarding the mask of how you think you should look and simply leading with the *authenticity* of who you are. At the heart of leading with authenticity is knowing and honoring your own *values*, while living and working with a clear sense of *purpose*. This alone can transform your life.

Deepening your liberation comes with **connecting**. All of your personal power and influence comes from your ability to connect with people. People are complex, which means traditional methods of controlling and bending them to your will can create disconnection, thereby limiting your power. You can raise your *impact* with people simply by *being present*. Being present consistently enough to affect the way people feel around you is what it means to *have presence*. Doing this requires that you disempower your *Inner Judge*, allowing *compassion* and *intimacy* to flourish in your relationships.

Fully liberated leadership is **taking responsibility** for your world. To even begin to take responsibility for your world, you must accept what is. *Accepting* the way things are—as opposed to *resisting* the way they are—is a more powerful starting point that allows you to act with true *response-ability*. It allows you to approach reality with a creative mindset instead of a victim mindset. The very essence of liberated leadership is *creating change*, whether in yourself, in the form of personal and professional growth, or in your environment—and being *present* and *aware* enough to *respond* creatively.

To do any of that requires *courage* and a willingness to be uncomfortable, because fear and the comfort of the status quo are strong forces. Practicing *liberated leadership* means being vulnerable and opening yourself up to discomfort. On the surface, this might seem counterintuitive to the idea of being happy. It's actually the opposite. While staying in your comfort zone can provide short-term pleasures and avoid short-term pain, true happiness is much deeper. Lasting happiness is sustained from within, not derived from something outside of you.

Choose happiness

In the end, I believe it's a choice to live your life in a certain way—a way that liberates you from Corporate Hell. It's not in the circumstances of your life that you find happiness, but in your *way of being* in relation to life. You can choose to show up in life as a leader. You can choose to take off the mask of trying to meet others' expectations all the time. You can choose the meaning of your life. You can begin to break down the barriers between you and the other humans around you, choosing compassion and connection, rather than judgment and separation. You can choose to take responsibility for your own life and career, regardless of what the world is throwing at you. You can choose your own actions, and even choose what you spend your time thinking about. In short, you can choose to live your life in the way that makes you happy, not miserable.

There is a ton of empirical research in the field of Positive Psychology that suggests happiness does not result from success. If you think about it, this makes sense. Do you think the people who have it all, in terms of worldly success, are universally happy? Conversely, are people with very few material possessions universally *unhappy*? The obvious answer in both cases is no. What the research suggests is the opposite—that success flows from happiness. That's right. We assume a cause and effect flowing from success to happiness, when in reality, it works the other way around. The implication for this is that we don't have to wait for anything or anyone in order to be happy.

After your last promotion, I'll bet you were happy. But how long did it last? I'm sure you quickly got used to it and then returned to your baseline level of happiness. The same is true for a pay raise, bonus, or job change. They're awesome to get, but in terms of making you happy, they have a severely limited shelf life. Career advancement will not lead you to lasting happiness. On the other hand, true happiness can provide the foundation for getting what you want out of your career. Don't focus on climbing the corporate ladder hoping for happiness. Focus instead on leading a happy, meaningful life and trust that you will create success in your career as a result.

If you're lucky, you'll get 80, 90, maybe even 100 years on this earth. When your time is up, how much of what you worried about during your life will really matter? If you knew you would die suddenly 7 days from now, I'm fairly certain you would change the way you spend the next 7 days. You already know with certainty you will die some-day. What do you want to look back on from your deathbed? If you want to look back with satisfaction, the time to create change is now. An old Chinese proverb says "The best time to plant a tree was 20 years ago. The second best time is now." Don't wait until it's too late.

Remember the final scene in the movie *Titanic*? Rose is on her deathbed and we're given a glimpse of the life she's lived since escaping fate on the sinking ship. In the pictures surrounding her bed, we see the evidence of a life fully lived, and she's surrounded by the people who loved her. I'll give you another movie reference. In *Braveheart*, the William Wallace character says: (imagine the Scottish accent) *"Every man dies. Not every man truly lives."*

In the grand scheme of your life, the things you allow to make corporate life hell are incredibly insignificant. Jobs are similar to life in one respect: they are both certain to end. Just as being on one's deathbed can provide perspective on life, so coming to the end of a career, or leaving a company, even leaving a job, can give us perspective. The things we worried so much about don't really matter. All of the successes and failures, the steps up the career ladder and the occasional step down or off, all of the joys and the frustrations—all of it is just material for experiencing a full life.

Be grateful for the opportunity.

BIBLIOGRAPHY AND SUGGESTED READINGS

Arbinger Institute. *Leadership and Self-Deception: Getting Out of the Box.* Berrett-Koehler Publishers, 2009.

Brown Brené. *Daring Greatly: How the Courage to Be Vulnerable Transforms the Way We Live, Love, Parent, and Lead.* Avery, 2012.

Carson, Rick. *Taming Your Gremlin: A Surprisingly Simple Method for Getting Out of Your Own Way.* HarperCollins Publishers, 2009.

Emerald, David. *The Power of TED*: *The Empowerment Dynamic.* Polaris Publishing, 2016.

Frankl, Viktor. *Man's Search for Meaning (New Edition).* Beacon Press, 2006.

Gallwey, W. Timothy. *The Inner Game of Work: Focus, Learning, Pleasure, and Mobility in the Workplace.* Random House, 2001.

Kabat-Zinn, Jon. *Full Catastrophe Living (Revised Edition): Using the Wisdom of Your Body and Mind to Face Stress, Pain, and Illness.* Bantam, 2013.

Kimsey-House, Karen. Kimsey-House, Henry. *Co-Active Leadership: Five Ways to Lead.* Berrett-Koehler Publishers, 2015.

Patterson, Kerry, et. al. *Crucial Conversations Tools for Talking When Stakes Are High, Second Edition.* McGraw-Hill Education, 2011.

Rock, David. *Your Brain at Work: Strategies for Overcoming Distraction, Regaining Focus, and Working Smarter All Day Long.* HarperCollins Publishers, 2009.

Ryan, Tim. *A Mindful Nation: How a Simple Practice Can Help Us Reduce Stress, Improve Performance, and Recapture the American Spirit.* Hay House, 2012.

Singer, Michael A. *The Untethered Soul: The Journey Beyond Yourself.* New Harbinger Publications, 2007.

Ware, Bronnie. *The Top Five Regrets of the Dying: A Life Transformed by the Dearly Departing.* Hay House, 2012.

GRATITUDE

This book emerged from a selfish choice. In pursuit of my dreams, I walked away from a healthy and (relatively) stable paycheck, and no one felt that more than my family. To my wife, Stephanie, I will be eternally grateful for your patience, encouragement, and seemingly never-ending belief in me. I love you. To my kids—Hannah, Niko, and Ty—you took it in stride when your dad's midlife career change threw a small wrench into your lives. I'm proud of you and grateful for the well-adjusted adults you are becoming. To my parents, Marlene and Terry, and my brother Chris with the "Atlanta Caracali," I'm grateful for all of your love.

I've had a lot of teachers in my life, formal and informal, and I'm grateful for every one of you. In particular, English teachers Glenn Ishiwata and Bruce Allen taught me how to write in my high school years. I still sometimes have your voices in my head when I'm editing and reading my own words. For Bill North, thank you for introducing me to Psychology in high school, before I knew I would someday study it.

In my internal corporate career I had twelve bosses over the course of twenty years. I've called more than one of you the "best boss I've ever had" at one point or another. Most of you did a fantastic job, and **all** of you taught me how important it is to put people first. Thank you for putting up with me.

In my twenty years of corporate life I attended countless training courses and leadership seminars and got to experience a wide range of instructors, facilitators, and leaders. From all of you I learned the art of connecting with those I seek to help, something I now do regularly and have strived to do in this book. Most recently, I've learned from two "Leaders Beside" in the Coaches Training Institute's Leadership Program—Henry Kimsey-House and Caroline Hall. Thank you for challenging me to step out of my comfort zone and grow. And to all the CTI faculty members who taught me to be the skilled coach that I am today, I thank you.

To the hundreds of leaders I've coached, trained, and led, and the thousands I've known throughout the years, thank you for trusting me, teaching me, and inspiring me. There is a piece of every one of you in me today.

I've never written a book until now, and I could not have done it without the support, guidance, and encouragement of so many people, too many to list here. I am grateful to each and every one of you for being in my life.

Thank you!

STAY CONNECTED

Join Mike's mailing list
www.CorporateLifeIsHell.com

WORK WITH MIKE

… as a speaker, to bring these ideas to life within your company or organization;

… as a leadership coach, to liberate the leader within you, raise your impact, and be happy in your life and your career;

… as a team coach, to transform your leadership team into a high performance team;

… as a facilitator, to help your team achieve breakthrough business results.

mikeCaracalas

LIBERATING LEADERS TO LEAD

www.MikeCaracalas.com

ABOUT MIKE

Mike Caracalas is a speaker, author, and executive leadership coach, liberating leaders to lead with courage, purpose, and love. He's lived the corporate life and continues to guide business leaders as they create a better world. Mike coaches individual leaders to become more happy, more effective, and more successful in their careers and he coaches ordinary teams to become high performance teams.

Mike lives in the Dallas/Fort Worth metroplex.

www.MikeCaracalas.com
www.CorporateLifeIsHell.com

 twitter.com/liberateleaders
 facebook.com/liberatedleadership

Made in the USA
Middletown, DE
05 April 2018